DELAYED 2
BUT NOT DENIED

Real Stories About
HOPE, FAITH, AND TRIUMPH

Book 2

D0830613

Compiled by
Toni Coleman Brown & Julia D. Shaw

DELAYED BUT NOT DENIED
Real Stories About Hope, Faith, and Triumph
Book 2

Published by Quantum Leap Productions LLC
444 Beach 22nd Street
Far Rockaway, NY 11691

www.networkforwomeninbusiness.com
www.shawbizconsulting.com
www.delayedbutnotdenied.info
www.thecollaborativeexperience.com

ISBN 978-0-9787568-3-3

Published in the United States

Book cover and Inside Layout:
Karine St-Onge
www.shinyrocketdesign.com

ACKNOWLEDGEMENT

Wow! I can hardly believe that we've completed another Delayed But Not Denied anthology. God is so good! I want to take this time to thank the authors who contributed to the second edition. This has to be one of the best compilation book projects I have participated in. Each story is priceless. Each author is unique and special in her own right. Special thanks to my partner in good, Julia Shaw. And a big thanks to Karine St-Onge of Shiny Rocket Design for her amazing design skills. Also, I could not do what I do without the most High God, so all praises to Him. And finally, I want to give all my family members a big shout out, especially Sasha, and Taylor.

Toni Coleman Brown

Toni and I are blessed to have our co-authors' voices of hope and healing in Delayed But Not Denied Book 1 and 2. Together we are a dream team come true! We acknowledge, love, and appreciate all of you. I thank God for my village of family and friends; my mom, sister Sherry and big baby brother Eddie, my daughters Asia Mya and Denisha Sherri; and my amazing grandchildren Kamari, Destiny, and Khloe. A special thanks to Toni Coleman Brown. We appreciate your faith and support in the Collaborative Experience. I love all y'all!

Julia D. Shaw aka "Julez"

TABLE OF CONTENTS

Compiled by **TONI COLEMAN BROWN** & **JULIA D. SHAW**

INTRODUCTION

After the success of our first book, *Delayed But Not Denied*, we knew we had to continue on this journey. We knew there were more stories like the ones we discovered in the first book. The *Delayed But Not Denied* series represents not only a vehicle of healing and transformation, but also a springboard for future careers for each author, who can use the book as a calling card for speaking engagements and an additional source of revenue. Just like in the first book, each co-author in Book 2 shares their bumps and potholes in this journey called life, with the hope of helping others avoid the same obstacles they have endured. And by chance, if any of the readers have hit the same potholes as our co-authors, they will know they are not alone and that there is sunlight at the end of the road.

In *Delayed But Not Denied 2* you will discover a fresh batch of stories that will inspire you, teach you, and let you know that life is a road that must be traveled all the way to the end. Situations that often start out as dark and scary, almost always end with light at the end of the tunnel, lessons learned, and unknown strengths found. All the stories hold true to the scripture, *Joy comes in the morning*. We have been encouraged and enlightened by every piece and we know that you will be as well.

We recommend that you read each chapter from beginning to end and then journal about how it has impacted you, and how you have been changed or encouraged by the author's words. This is the reason why we have left a few blank pages in the back of the book for notes.

We want you to journal and to express your truth. We also want to encourage you to begin the process of writing your own *Delayed But Not Denied* story. If you have experienced a difficult or life-changing situation and overcame it in a major way; this may be just the opportunity for you. We would like to invite you to participate in *Delayed But Not Denied: Book 3*. If you are interested in contributing to our next project, please visit www. delayedbutnotdenied.info to discover how you can become a bestselling author in our next book. In the meantime, we hope that you are blessed by these stories as much as we have been.

As sisters in business, we are driven to help others succeed at their purpose and make their dreams of becoming bestselling authors come true.

Passionately,
Toni Coleman Brown & Julia D. Shaw

ABOUT

Maria Dowd

Maria Dowd is a motivational speaker, author and trailblazing entrepreneur who speaks at conferences, seminars, and book talks throughout the U.S., as well as in the West Indies and Central America.

Her life took a dramatic turn after a divorce in 2012. It was a huge wakeup call, as Maria—as so many women do—faced the reality that she had fallen into the trappings of financial co-dependency. It was time to reboot her life.

In winter of 2015, Maria recognized that her psyche was more bruised than she'd realized. She began charting her very uncomfortable realities, then designed what she dubbed **My Amazing LYFE MAP**—now an interactive e-course of bold, insightful challenges, vision boarding, and rewards that helps women flip indecisiveness, unsteadiness, and heartache into elevated levels of self-awareness, self-activism, and transformation.

Maria founded and produced African American Women on Tour (AAWOT)—known as the foremost women's empowerment conference series—from 1991 to 2003. It attracted over 30,000 women and teens worldwide.

After retiring AAWOT, Maria represented a line of botanical self-care products, and led a direct sales organization of over 1,000 consultants. She authored three inspirational books: *Journey to Empowerment, Journey into My Brother's Soul, and Journey to a Blissful Life*, which was featured in *Essence* magazine, as one of the best books on personal renewal. For five years, Maria operated San Diego's exclusive Design Essentials distributorship, representing its professional line of hair care solutions.

Maria is a native Californian, a mom to two daughters, and "Mimi" to her delightful five-year-old grandson. She enjoys travel, Zumba, independent films, and thrift store shopping.

Email:	maria@MyAmazingLYFE.com
Phone:	619-750-8232
Websites:	www.MyAmazingLYFE.com www.MyMoneyLYFE.com
Facebook:	MariaDeniseDowd MyAmazingLYFE MyMoneyLYFE
Instagram:	maria.myamazinglyfe
Twitter:	AmazingLYFEMap
LinkedIn:	mariadowd

MY AMAZING LIFE EVOLVING

By Maria Dowd

It was April, 2012.

We were sitting in the audience, among maybe five hundred women and thirty men. Most were entrepreneurs. The scene was so familiar it made me shudder. People were on their feet, whooping and hollering. The motivational speaker, Lisa Nichols, had stirred all this up.

I should have felt the same elation as a woman, and an entrepreneur. Instead, I felt an intense heartache. Next up was a mini parade of well-dressed women, each with personal testimonials everyone in the room could relate to. Listening to them I became even sadder, and ever-so-slightly envious. Okay. Maybe the envy wasn't so slight. They all seemed so unbridled, free to be, do, say, and dance in their respective Universes—fearlessly and unapologetically defiant. Goddess, Wild Woman, Amazon, Free Spirit all came to mind, as I absorbed each word of their fascinating success stories. Maybe I was reading more into the scene, but I felt irritated and numb. In that moment, I was challenged with finding any of those descriptions within my own soul.

All right, pull it together. Don't start crying, Maria.

What was going on inside that ballroom was *my* gig...once upon a time. I was instrumental in creating these same kinds of frenzied spaces, when the likes of Iyanla Vanzant, Bertice Berry, and Susan L. Taylor hit my stages in every major city across the U.S. During my thirteen-year journey as the Founder and Producer of African American Women on Tour (AAWOT) a trailblazing women's empowerment conference, I brought together the best and the brightest African-American female motivational speakers, celebrities, coaches, trainers, authors, mentors and spiritual leaders—as a unified community brimming with love, wisdom and Amazon-like fierceness. How in the f*ck did I get into this emotionally erratic space? I had morphed into a woman resigned to playing small and safe. I'd gotten lost in a toxic situation that left very little wiggle room for being my authentic self. My daughters spotted it right away, and were very vocal about it. Close friends stepped more gingerly around this shift in the way I was showing up in the world. And I… well… I minimized their perspectives, while rationalizing my own.

I had to escape from that conference room, filled with so many happy women. I'd become very familiar with "flight"—the art of shutting down. I had close to a decade of practice. I learned how to fly away from loud, vicious insults when I was deemed "out of line." If I were lucky, it happened over the phone. I'd simply put down my phone—nonstop rantings still spewing out of the mouthpiece—and leave the room.

Today, a chord was struck, one that had been on lockdown for quite some time. I was done pretending. It took being surrounded by exuberance for that long-closed door to finally open. I had to leave the conference room to find a quiet place to download… and to sob. Today would be a marker, my line in the sand. No more eggshell walking. No more boundaries crossed. No more fretting over upsetting that damn, three-wheeled apple cart.

I found an empty bathroom, locked myself inside the handicap stall, and tumbled into a soggy, muffled breakdown, only a few feet away from the room once comfortably air-conditioned, likely now a sweat lodge. Each salty tear drop contained a familiar emotion—regret, resignation, discontent and distress, colored by fear and melancholy.

I knew the moment I stepped out of that public restroom would be the beginning of my breakthrough. I'd run out of decorum. I was not going to return to my seat and surrender to unhappiness. I was going to take a stand for myself… *no matter what. I* choose. My "flight" wings were now officially retired.

After a few deep breaths, I reapplied my favorite chili matte lipstick. My eyeliner was wrecked along with the tissue it stained. My brain was now shifting into strategic planning mode. I *needed* to figure out how to become a part of *this* community. My entire being was calling for liberation. I needed breathing room. I needed a scrutiny-free, judgement-free zone to rediscover the beloved woman I'd been slowly strangling. I needed connection with people who lived in gardens of possibilities and opportunities; not wastelands of insecurities and threats. Those few moments inside the ballroom awakened something in me. I knew this was my pivot point. It was time to remove myself from the no-win cat-and-mouse game I'd been forced to play. It was either revival or survival.

After leaving the restroom, I looked for the woman who had graciously invited me to this event. I would have to convince her that I was qualified to once again be a part of that most elite community of entrepreneurs—the ones who had invested close to $40K to be a part of it. I *maybe* had $40 in my business checking account in that moment. What would it hurt to ask? I hadn't considered the "how." I only knew that I needed to surround myself with creators, dealmakers, rock stars, and ambassadors of transformation, to refuel my soul.

When I walked out, there she was... less than twenty feet away, in a conversation with another woman. I waited. When she was alone, I approached. I told her about my past work in women's empowerment, and shared that Lisa, the motivational speaker, would likely remember me. She assured me that she would follow up, and see what was possible. I thanked and hugged her.

Returning to the ballroom, it was quieter now. I took my seat, took a deep breath and declared:

"I need to be a part of this community... and I need for you (the old me) to *NOT* be a part of this community."

A few months later, I got a call. It was a request to volunteer for Lisa Nichol's fall event. I was elated. My marriage was rapidly dissolving. We were amicable, at least until I asked for financial help, while I figured out what was next for me. That's when the wall went up.

My business situation was unmanageable. After being brought onboard as a new distributor operating under an untested business model, I landed in a financial obligation that turned into what essentially became sharecropping. The more product I sold, the deeper into a chasm I fell, trying to keep up with a demand that I'd created, while trying to pay down a never-ending debt. I was surrounded by rabbit holes I had to figure my way around.

Fortunately, I had my loving family and a new entrepreneurial family. They provided support and accountability. There were also those in-my-face daughter-mother pep talks. And the volunteer role that advanced into a paid staff position. In the backdrop, a bankruptcy and surprising contested divorce ensued, as I prepared for my mother to move in with me. It was a surreal time in my life. I quietly watched, learned, and served new circles of dynamic individuals, doing powerful and positive work in the world. I was making my way back, one tiny, yet bold step at a time.

I was still at odds with reconciling my cash flow requirements and mounting legal expenses with my quest to rediscover what my true north would look like twenty-five years post-African American Women on Tour. I dipped my toe in here and there, seeking that "something" that would ignite my *élan vital*… my life force. Each experience—while not the ultimate answer—was surely a piece of a bigger blueprint.

A certified coach and long-time friend of mine suggested I take an assessment that would help point me in the right direction. I took it, skimmed over the findings, and set it aside. I dismissively noted that I was—hands-down—a *creator*: visionary, creative, optimistic, stimulating, able to inspire others, can multitask, quick to get results, and great at getting things started. And, secondarily, a *mechanic*: completes things, finds ways to improve systems, makes things simpler, perfects projects, pays attention to details; along with a *star*: creative, outgoing, able to motivate and inspire others, quick to connect, holds the stage, high energy and knows how to have fun. *Intuitive thinker*. Okay. Got it. This revelation would be tabled until further notice. I had a new job and a bucket load of legal matters to tend to.

Over the next three years, I watched, listened, and flexed my entrepreneurial muscle. I got the opportunity to pinpoint the many things that went awry in my past business enterprises. I was beginning to know now what I didn't know then. I was afforded the privilege to work behind those velvet curtains, and inside boardrooms. I garnered the best practices from masterful business owners. I also became even more attuned to our human-ness, and our tendency to often be out of sync with our *whole Self*. What crystallized for me? We can be batting 100 percent financially, but our emotional well-being is hovering around the lower percentile range. We might wear the finest $450 power dress, and be operating at a 14 percent self-esteem capacity. We may publicly perpetrate a glorious love relationship but—behind the scenes—it's clouded with madness.

I became this vocational gypsy, roaming in and out of opportunities, constantly asking myself those three critical "hedgehog" questions, a la author, Jim Collins:

1. What lights my fire?

2. What could I be best in the world at?

3. What will make me money?

I knew that I went to sleep each night, and woke up each morning, thinking about how I might touch the life of a woman who felt frustrated, overwhelmed, undervalued or disrespected. And, now I was increasingly thinking about the best, and most impactful ways to become a part of her extended family of expert coaches and advocates, to guide and support her; to help advance her thinking, strength, and capacity to play full out in her life.

During my journey with AAWOT we touched the hearts and souls of over 30,000 women. It became quite clear, the elements that worked that I could duplicate; and the ones that didn't work and should not be duplicated, and the impact of both. I promised myself to create an enterprise founded in working smarter, instead of harder.

The way I managed AAWOT didn't leave much income for me. While serving those who came to AAWOT—seeking answers, to share their genius, and expand their enterprises—I did a lousy job of taking care of my present and future financial needs. Losing myself in day-to-day operational stuff, I overlooked the need to build something that would sustain me and my family, during and post-AAWOT. Instead, I burned myself out... then walked away, pretty much penniless.

While all of these positive shifts were taking place in my life, I was still going toe to toe with that teeny weeny, disruptive voice—inside my head—that was telling me I was "wrong" for my past missteps and errors in judgement. And, I still had to address a few unhealthy "self-preservation" habits I'd created... that certainly wouldn't serve me in my new life. A friend noticed the stark absence of photos of myself on Facebook. In my former life, "just me" posts would have been distorted into something crude... with consequences.

I set out to tackle this "thing" head on. I discovered a timely fifty-four—minute sermon literally entitled "Curing Regret" by Pastor Toure Roberts.

Perfect! A simple, five-step formula:

1. Understand what it is, the error of it, and the harm it causes.

2. Pause and take inventory of how much time you have been wasting while regretting.

3. Let regret die under the light of God's love, mercy and plan to restore and prosper you.

4. If possible, create a do-over.

5. Move on.

I listened. I cried. I released... then I moved on for good.

Now it was time to take a different kind of inventory, this time of my current realities. While it was a little uncomfortable at first, splashing my feet around in *transparency* was incredibly refreshing. They included my lack of consistent cash flow, insufficient retirement savings, sporadic exercising, and a marginal social and networking life. Once I had a complete picture of where and how I was shortchanging myself, it was easier to plug in goals and milestones, and ensure that my goals were aligned with my core life values: *vitality, self-expression, wealth, contribution, and contentment.*

I then wrote this personal manifesto:

This is absolutely the most prosperous, exciting and happiest time of my life.
I'm the Shining Star of my Life in its Entirety.
I'm achieving all of my personal and business goals.
I'm overflowing with comfort, optimal health, and gratitude.
I'm living in whole, perfect, and complete harmony, and love.
And, I'm a catalyst for my own and others' transformational journey.

Everything that was of highest importance to me, pours from me. As I spanned all twelve "channels" of my life, I integrated affirming words and images onto each page. These images morphed into mini vision boards that deeply resonated with me. Then, I gave it a name—**My Amazing LYFE Map**. It became an ever-evolving, course-correcting examination and composition of my *whole* life, including my emotions, physical well-being, money, love, family, spirituality, my social life, and entrepreneurial journey; as well as the legacy I wanted to leave behind.

Every month I visit my life map, I ask myself:

1. What do I REALLY want?

2. Are these choices truly mine, and mine alone?

3. Have I taken the time to survey the landscape and possible pitfalls?

4. What's the wisest path to getting there?

5. What's required of me to stay on purpose, improve my genius, and sustain myself financially?

During one of my trips to Los Angeles to hang out with my thirty-something-year-old daughters; after my grandson Noah was tucked in, my daughters and I exchanged updates on our personal and professional lives. It was a safe space. As usual with these two, I was awed not only by their very mature levels of insight, but also their unwavering certainty about their entrepreneurial goals and aspirations. My eldest daughter showed me her life map—a different format but same principle. It was my turn. I shared where I was, and how I wanted to fulfill my women's empowerment mission during this season of my life. They grew up in African American Women on Tour, so they understood. My daughters not only showered me with their thoughts and suggestions, they pulled out paper and pencil and further refined my vision. It felt like a homecoming. I went to bed with a huge smile on my heart.

I embraced and celebrated my ever-emerging clarity. The Universe started presenting new possibilities. I did a lot of decluttering—within my physical, mental, and emotional environments. For the first time in my life, I began dating men of different races and cultural backgrounds. I was exercising more consistently, and getting regular full-body massages. These were just a few of the promises I'd made to myself... and was keeping.

The truest test came when I shared a snapshot of my map on Facebook. I was delighted to find women asking for guidance on creating their own life maps. I answered the call with the creation of the **My Amazing LYFE Map e-Course. LYFE: Live-Your-Freedom-Everyday!** This highly engaging instructional platform offers tools, challenges, activities, and journaling that can help move anyone who's ready—out of that gray mass of unsteadiness, uncertainty, and distress into amazing clarity and expanded feelings of well-being and freedom.

The biggest lessons learned:

- There is no "curing" one area, and leaving disharmony and imbalance in other areas unchecked. The holistic approach is ideal.

- Know your divinely appointed mission on this planet, in this lifetime. Living outside of our purpose can keeps us in survival mode.

- Recognize, utilize, and sharpen your natural gifts; leverage them to profoundly transform lives, especially your own.

- Listen to your intuition, and look out for potential detours and derailments of your game plans.

- Seek enlightened counsel and mentoring. Expand your circles to include people who are wiser, and more successful than you.

- Express self-love through self-care. Fold them into your life on a daily basis. Self-care is yielding to, and celebrating *your* well-being.

- Never fear asking for what you need and want. There's value and opportunity in every yes, no, and maybe you get. Appreciate it all.

- A life map keeps us moving in our *appointed* direction, and aligned with *our* core values. It creates a straighter, more congruent course.

Finally, there's nothing like sharing, building community, and celebrating with other like minds and spirits. The beauty of this journey is that it is ever-evolving. The "finished" product is never finished. The journey is about self-awareness, inspiration, and self-activism. In the process, we get more energized, gain a stronger voice, more freedom, and the confidence to get what we need and want out of life.

―――――― ABOUT ――――――
Julie Ann Fairley

Julie Ann Fairley is an elementary school teacher in the New York City public school system. She is the author of a short story and book of poems for children titled, *Coco, Rainbow, Cherry, Mango Flavors for Friends*. She has also written for a magazine called, *Women of Power*. Fairley just completed *I'll Let You Know*, her first book of poems for the adult market. She is currently working on a greeting card line for children that addresses their various concerns. As a writer, Fairley felt the need to become the voice of the young people's joy, pain, and struggles. Fairley believes that as much as things have changed, many of the life lessons she learned as a child remain the same.

Julie Ann received her B.A. Degree and M.S. in Education from Herbert H. Lehman College in the Bronx, NY. She is the mother of three daughters and her late son. Fairley is a lover of life and all its possibilities. As the late author, J. California Cooper profoundly wrote, "The matter is life…" Keeping this in mind, Julie Ann embraces it all!

Email:	kumpanee55@gmail.com
Facebook:	Author Julie Ann Fairley or julie.fairley.94.

ALL THAT I AM

By Julie Ann Fairley

It was December 24th Christmas Eve, and we hadn't seen Mommy in two whole days. Well, almost two because she came in once, for a few minutes, and put a brown paper bag on the kitchen table. When she went into the bathroom I hurried to the table and took out the contents of the bag. Out came the Franco American canned spaghetti, a loaf of Wonder Bread, a package of Spiced Ham, and two containers of milk. There was also a paper plate with a huge hump, wrapped in Aluminum Foil. Inside, was a hunk of somebody's birthday cake. Anytime Ma was gone for a day or two, she returned home with somebody's birthday cake, for us. Always. Ma used to come home with drooping eyelids and skin that lacked shine. She was often very tired and depressed because she had little to no money. She worked as a Bar Maid and a cook in a place called the "Trinity Bar" on Boston Road in The Bronx. Oftentimes, people celebrated their birthdays there, while listening to the juke box, playing pool and dancing in the center of the floor. Me, as inquisitive as I was, had ventured into the place looking for her at one time or another...She always gave me some wrapped up food to take back to the house and dared me to come out again.

Our Bronx apartment in the old wooden house was not very warm. The huge living room was partitioned off by a long brown dresser; giving us a space against a wall for a twin bed, and another space, right across, for the fold-up cot, which was hardly ever folded. The apartment was a disaster; littered with dirty clothes mixed with clean clothes, ashtrays filled with cigarette butts, and old TV guides. There were empty coffee cups and Pepsi Cola cans scattered around. Toy trucks without wheels, a headless walk-with-me doll and broken crayons were all over the living room. And the twins—six-year-old boys—were doing anything they felt like doing. They turned on the TV switching the channels back and forth; rode their tricycles on top of the clothes on the floor; dug into the Peanut Butter jar and licked spoons full like ice cream. They even tried fixing our old rabbit eared TV antennae with a butter knife, desperately trying to get a clearer picture. When they got tired of all that, they'd tie undershirts on their heads—pretending to be pirates—and play fight. It was my job to watch them. Period. I was ten years old.

I often did that from an old, flowered armchair in a corner of the room. The seat was sunken and the back was not quite plump, its cotton filling peeking from a small tear. The chair soothed me. I rocked myself, front and back; banging my back into the cushion—sometimes fast, sometimes slow. I made up songs and sang then to myself. My first song was always the "Mommy Song." "I want my mommy, I want my mommy, I want my mother to come home." I'd sing and sing, rocking and banging my back into the cushion. Faster and faster, then slower and slower I rocked until I got sick of myself, and that "done for nothing" song. The song was just that… "done for nothing" although each time I sang it, I did so with the hope that she'd come through the door. The song usually left me wondering, scared, and feeling alone; sitting in a mess that wasn't my own.

I made up stories, loud stories, any kind of story to get the twins to sit down. They would too, for a little while and they were even quiet. One sucked his thumb, spit shining it. The other just stared at me; his lazy eye, wandering toward the bridge of his nose, made him look puzzled. At least I had their attention. I'd found a way to make them listen to me; their ten-year old sister.

When I got tired of all the singing, rocking, and storytelling, I looked around the dingy apartment; at the gray ceiling overhead and the hanging plaster pieces from a nearby wall with exposed wooden slats. The twins had started digging their own holes in one of the walls—they'd found a way to see outside into the hallway. The dull flowered wallpaper, at one time—way before my time—must've been beautiful to somebody. But that had to have been ages ago. As I sat, "I don't care" settled in, and over me.

I tried to perk up the place by drawing penciled tulips, and crayoned flowers and taping them to the walls. I went back to where I was sitting, my place to rock—to my back and forth world. My world of faster, faster, and slower, slower. I wanted to fix this place—this raggedy old house! I wanted to change *everything*—I wanted it clean! I wanted Mommy home. I wanted Grandma to come back from Florida. I wanted Jimboy to come back from his father's house in Queens. I wanted the warmth of Auntie's Stephen Foster apartment to surround me. I wanted to sit inside, on the windowsill, with Uncle Jimmy's binoculars and stare out into a world far away from 163rd Street and Caldwell Avenue. I wanted to see way past the top of Morris High School. I wanted... Christmas carols and wooden soldiers, sugar cookies, and Santa Claus... I wanted new clothes... I wanted my father! I wanted to go outside and not be picked on because I lived in an old house. I wanted... I wanted...

I jumped up, out of my thoughts and decided, in an instant, that I was going to do something right then and there about the house. Our silver Christmas tree was in a box that was stuffed in back of the closet, way behind some old boots and shoes. I knew how to set it up; put the long silver poles together, spread out the three-legged stand and stick in the poles, then put in the silver aluminum branches. Yeah, that was it! Decorations? None. I didn't care though because Santa was coming through the door. If he didn't—as much as I tried to force myself to believe in magic; to believe in the promise of "Santa Claus is coming to town"—something would be different. I decided when I woke up the next morning, if there wasn't proof that Santa had come, I'd have to face the truth—that magic doesn't exist. I already knew the truth, but I wanted to feel something *good*, something other than that sinking feeling I carried most of the time.

I went into the only closet in the apartment. It was pretty big, and as I pushed and dug through old coats and taped boxes, I came across a beautiful, musical photo album. It was black and shiny with hand-painted palm trees, and small pink and green flowers on the front and back. I twisted the metal wind-up key and soft music played. I opened the album and between the pages were tissue paper and pictures of Jimboy holding the twins. There was a black and white picture of me at five holding Derek (he had gotten sick and died in the house with me when he was seven) staring out into the world. There were school pictures, a baby photo of me, and pictures of some people I didn't know. I held the album very carefully, then I put it back inside its box and wrapped the box back inside the towel I'd found it in. My next thought was, *clean up the mess in the house!*

There was no hot water. I had no memory of warm water ever coming out of the faucet. It was always ice cold. For hot water I had to boil some in the two big pots that were kept on the shelf. I had to be "super careful." I'd heard Mommy say that the old house would burn up quickly because it was mostly wood. That was the main reason she didn't want me trying to cook. But I'd watched her many times when she'd take a long wooden match out the matchbox, strike it on the side of the box—turn on the gas stove and "whoosh!" A burst of flames appeared. Then she'd turn down the flame. Shoot, I knew how to do it! And once, after I told her I knew how to do it, she let me light the stove in front of her. She warned me not to let my clothes get close to the flames, to wet the used match stick in water before throwing it away, and to never, *ever* throw a match stick into the garbage thinking it was out! "This house will burn like hell!" she said.

Mommy knew I could do it—that's why she'd buy Campbell's Chicken Noodle Soup or cans of Spaghetti and Meatballs because she knew, her queen (as she called me) could heat up food and take care of the twins until she came home.

There was a feeling inside of me that day. It was pounding in the tiniest part of me, microscopic. It pushed me—I didn't know exactly to where. One thing was for sure—I was a collection of all the good I'd ever seen, all the bad I'd seen, and of all my wants and dreams. In an instant, I became strong and powerful; able to clean up the incredible mess we lived in. I had to make something good happen. I stood in the center of the room, looking around. *What should I do first?* I thought. *Clear it all out!* That's what I'd do. I'd sweep the floor and make a great big pile. Separate the garbage from the clothes and anything else that was important. Throw the garbage away after the floor was swept. Then wash the dishes and pots. The kitchen... Oh my goodness, it was in bad shape! Everything was piled up in the sink—crusty bowls, empty glass jars, pots, forks, and spoons. I inched closer and looked at the kitchen floor—old linoleum, with big, black, patches of worn out red diamond shapes, was curled up around the edges. *How was I going to get all this cleaning done before Christmas?* I wondered. *I know, I'd put all the dirty pots and pans in the bathtub and boil some pots of water to pour over them. Then I'd let them soak while I washed the others in the kitchen sink.*

I heard the twins—one laughed as the other said, "You stupid, Ju!" They came into the kitchen and ran circles around me. "What you lookin' for Ju? Candy?" I shook my head. I then looked at them and said, "If you sit down and watch TV while I clean up, I'll go to the store and get some Tootsie Rolls and Sugar Babies." I then sweetened the deal. "And if you're *extra* good, I'll get some Wise Potato Chips." In response, the twins ran into the living room and sat in front of the TV. I didn't have a dime, but if I went next door to Mr. Jeff's Candy Store, he'd give it to me on credit because he knew Ma! He also knew she probably wasn't home.

As I cleaned, the twins happily sat on the floor in front of the TV counting their Sugar Babies. I'd already swept everything into the middle of the room, so I put what I thought was trash in the garbage can; which included cups filled with cigarette butts, old newspapers, and a ripped, black half-slip. I then threw all the clothes in the closet. The pile in front of me was getting smaller as the stack in the closet got larger. I stopped for a few seconds to see where I would put the twins' tricycles. I really wanted the house to look nice. I'd told them to make sure they put them against the wall when they finished riding them so I'd find them easily. They nodded in agreement, said, "Okay Ju," and went back to watching *Felix The Cat*. Next thing I knew, after all that bending and sorting and stuffing—it was done! The living room/bedroom was spic and span. Gee! Ten-year-old me had done it!

I'd gotten myself two Payday candy bars instead of Sugar Babies. I loved caramel and peanuts! I ate half of one and put the rest on top of the refrigerator. It was time to get to work on the kitchen. It was warm now 'cause the steam from the boiling water filled the air. I was kinda scared to lift the big pot; so, I used a towel and carefully grabbed the handles, (something I'd seen Mommy do). I cautiously removed it from the stove and walked slowly over to the sink. I ran some cold water into the pot, not too much though. I picked up the bar of Octagon Soap and dropped it in the water. I hated that soap! It wasn't bubbly enough, but it didn't matter 'cause I had to use it. After swooshing it around in the water and rubbing it against the dishcloth, I went into the bathroom to get some pots out of the tub. I tracked a lot of water to the sink, but finally, *finally* I got the job done. I left a huge black roasting pan in the tub; scooped out all the soggy food and sprinkled Ajax around the greasy ring that was left. I then stood in the kitchen doorway, taking in all the work I'd done *all by myself*. I was so proud. The job was almost done… The Christmas tree was next—I had to put it together.

I wanted a real tree; a *huge* real tree that made the house smell good, like at Auntie's house. And I wanted it to have different colored bulbs and strings of lights that flickered all around. I'd asked Mommy for one and she said, "Hell no! Girl this old ass house will burn down if the tree gets dried out and the electric bulbs get hot." That was the end of that. All we had was an aluminum tree with most of its branches bent, a silver star for the top, and no decorations. The ornaments had gotten broken and never replaced. I didn't care though— up went the tree in the center of the room. It was crooked and sparse; but it was the shiniest thing in the house. I closed my eyes and prayed for a Santa Claus that I knew would not come. The thought of there being Santa magic made things easier to think about for a few minutes. I prayed big prayers—I prayed for something that would be different and make things better. When I opened my eyes, I decided that when I grew up, I'd live in a place where things would be clean, that I would have money, and that I would *somehow, someway* make good things happen for anyone who I met, who felt like me.

It had been very quiet for a while. The twins must've fallen asleep on each other in front of the TV. I walked into the living room and picked them up, one at a time and put them on the cot. One at the top, the other at the bottom. I covered them with a blanket and a coat to keep them extra warm. I was so, so tired. I sat on the other cot and lay down in my clothes. I had left the television and every light in the house on; and had dragged the silver tree into another part of the house. If anything was different when I opened my eyes, I'd know that Mommy was home.

I didn't sleep well. I woke up for a few minutes and stared at the brightly lit ceiling. "She ain't here." I said to myself. Everything was quiet. I knew it was too early to get up because the twins were asleep. It was still dark outside, I could tell from the curtains. I rolled over and went back to sleep with the invisible sinking feeling and the thought that Ma wouldn't be home when I got up. Merry Christmas.

The next time I opened my eyes, it was daylight. The twins were still asleep. *Good*, I thought. I sat on the bed and looked around the room. All the lights were still on. I tiptoed through the apartment and turned out the lights. I went into the kitchen hoping there was a can of Carnation Milk and enough Quaker Oats to make breakfast for the three of us; there was. I knew how to make the oatmeal smooth and creamy. I sucked in all the air I could, hoping somehow to let out the sinking feeling that lived inside me with my next breath. It didn't happen.

There were no gifts for us on that day. When Ma returned home, I was just so happy that I was able to do something to make her smile. While the gifts did not happen, what did happen, was I became aware that I could make changes in my life. All I needed was the desire, determination, and a willingness to do the hard work. I knew, no matter the difficulties and the sinking feeling I often carried, that I also carried feelings of self-satisfaction and pride. I also carried love, goodness, and dreams. One thing was for sure; that Christmas Eve let me know that I had the ability to make changes and to make good things happen. That little girl lives inside me still and is at the core of all that I am.

ABOUT

Rev. Dr. Cheryl Y. James

Rev. Dr. Cheryl Y. James is a respected woman of God, a Christian chaplain, and a humble servant who desires to inspire and is committed to supporting women and children with cancer, baldness, and low self-esteem because of appearance-related concerns. She continues to guide those who are afflicted and low in spirit, through her organizations Where There's A Need Inc., and Cheryl James Consulting. Her heart is expertly guided by a noble purpose and an altruistic sense of humanity, in accordance with II Timothy 2:24. *I am she; a gentle servant of the Lord, a teacher, with patience and humility.*

Her desire is to support total wellness of mind, body, and spirit, and to serve the community at large. Charity and love produces a sense of peace and fulfillment. She believes that, it does take a village and to whom much is given, much is required.

Dr. James' vision is to continue to embody the spirit of service!

Address:	P.O. Box 310998 Jamaica, N.Y. 11432
Phone:	718-529-3638
Website:	www.wheretheresaneed.org
Email:	charitee123@yahoo.com
Facebook:	cherylyjames
LinkedIn:	cheryljames123

FROM ORDINARY TO EXTRAORDINARY

By Rev. Dr. Cheryl Y. James

*I am she, a gentle servant of the Lord,
a teacher with patience and humility.*

— II Timothy 2:24

Life always offers us a multitude of choices. From childhood to adulthood, we have been afforded opportunities and given options, directions, and instructions that shape our decision-making skills. The possibilities are endless. To be or not to be?

The desire to offer assistance will kick in because our understanding of service will be evident. Serving others does not require large amounts of money. It only requires a willing heart and spirit.

When we think of the word *ordinary*, we understand that this thinking or behavior, usually offers nothing extra. It's merely a regular routine out of habit. It's your usual, normal, standard, typical, common behavior, providing no mountaintop experience. However, when we think of the word *extraordinary*, we understand that this thinking or behavior is usually considered *very* unusual or even remarkable. This behavior and thinking can also be considered exceptional, sensational, unbelievable and even phenomenal, and usually provides a mountaintop experience.

When we go out of our way, or leave our comfort zone in order to become an extraordinary presence in the life of someone who may feel helpless, hopeless, downtrodden, and destitute, we enter into a God ordained realm, as a Christian. The desire to do something, feels like we are representing God on earth. This realm can allow one to fulfill their purpose. It can feel like a place of grace, satisfaction, fulfillment and even joy.

I remember when I first felt this feeling. Over fifteen years ago my daughter's second grade classmate and good friend suffered a brain aneurism. The ordeal was understandably overwhelming for the little girl. A team of doctors had to perform brain surgery to stop the bleeding in her brain. The surgery was lengthy and her head had to be shaved. Her recuperation was challenging. When my daughter called her little friend, the child asked if she could please come and visit her at home.

As I listened to their phone conversation, I heard the little girl express a concern she had about returning to school. She was afraid to go back to school because of her shaved head. Her fear was that she would be teased by classmates and students. She was uncomfortable with her appearance. My heart sank as I pondered what kind of gift we could bring her. She had a specific need and worry. A baby doll or board game would not suffice. This little girl was low in spirit, self-esteem, and had an appearance related concern. The Lord spoke to my heart and gave me an idea.

I always had a love for hair and makeup and although I didn't attend cosmetology school I was good at it. It was just a God-given gift and talent I thoroughly enjoyed doing in my spare time. I followed God's lead and began to dismantle one of my wigs. I had a brand new yellow scarf I had recently purchased for my daughter. I cut up the wig and attached parts of it to the beautiful yellow scarf to make a thick black bang in the front. When I was finished I'd created my first wig alternative.

My daughter and I then visited the child hoping she would love what I had created for her. As I placed it on her head, she smiled and was amazed that you couldn't tell the attached bang was not her real hair. Her face lit up with miles of smiles. She could now return to school without worry or concern. This gift was more than just wig and a scarf. It gave her a sense of self-esteem and restored the very thing she'd been robbed of. It addressed the very concern she was worried about, which was her appearance. This awesome gift allowed her to return to school with confidence and look like every other little girl.

She was the inspiration for my organization, Where There's A Need, Inc.

We have been dressing and addressing the heads of women and girls with baldness, of every age and nationality, for the past fifteen years. I am also proud to hold a copyright and patent for the hair scarf design, which allows our organization to address the possibility of infringement.

It's unfortunate that cancer treatment can lead to baldness, along with the diagnoses of hair loss from alopecia, and many other medical conditions. For this cause, our organization will always be a resource for these patients. I take pride in the ability to create special hairstyles for children, and to address the need of limited affordable hair loss coverings for girls and teens. I am also appreciative for the opportunity and tools to create exclusive wig alternative styles for communities of color, and inner-city patients, which consist of: braids, curls, dreadlocks, ponytails, afros and other ethnic hairstyles.

Serving others, can bring joy and satisfaction, but also challenges, and sadness. The quest to serve this targeted audience has allowed me the opportunity to visit many cancer centers in four of the five boroughs of New York City and donate items to many who have limited finances. The memories and stories will be a consistent reminder of the need to serve others and offer works of charity.

While visiting a Brooklyn hospital cancer center, I had the pleasure of meeting two sisters who were undergoing cancer chemotherapy treatment. They told me that they were EMS workers and on 9/11 were directed to The World Trade Center in an effort to save lives. Here they are today each with a cancer diagnosis, and in need of treatment to save *their* lives. The women asked if they could have a wig alternative and were so grateful for any form of support that we could offer.

Eight years ago I received a phone call from a young mother with cancer. She was in her thirties, and married with two small children. She was unable to wear wigs because she had major scalp irritation and soreness. She was also troubled and heartbroken that her young children had to see her sick and without hair. One of them would stare at her and ask, "Why does Mommy look like Daddy." This was obviously very difficult for her, and she was hopeful that I could create something that her scalp could handle, that would also allow her to feel pretty. When she received our package she was beyond happy. Her husband and friends expressed their gratitude and mentioned how less sick and more like herself she looked. Hearing this made my day. My heart is thrilled for every opportunity to be of service to so many women and girls who desire to be uplifted, supported, and able to function in society with their illness undetected.

My wonderful experiences don't stop there. I recall a nine-year-old child with cancer who I created ponytails for. I would visit her at home and spend time with her while her mom was at work. We watched cartoons together and I taught her how to make gingerbread houses. She was so funny and full of energy in spite of her illness. One day she told me that her form of cancer was Leukemia and that she couldn't find any orange cancer ribbons, only pink. I went to the nearest fabric store and purchased orange ribbon and created a special cancer ribbon just for her. The little darling called me every week to ask for dreadlocks and other hairstyles. I asked her why she wanted dreadlocks, and she said because her mom wore them.

Then there was the mother of a four-year-old girl who asked for a pink scarf with a brown bang and curls. I visited her as well and realized that because of her young age, she could care less about being bald, and fortunately, she didn't notice the stares from people when they were out in public. But it was clear that her mom was uncomfortable with them. This helped me to realize and understand that parents of children with illness are also in need of support.

Last, there was a six-year-old girl who had alopecia and downs syndrome. Her mother requested a white scarf with blond bangs and curls. They were both so excited and happy with the wig alternative that her mother sent me a photo of the little girl wearing it. She asked me to display it on our website to encourage other families.

I am committed to a life of service and fulfilling the mission of our organization. As a Christian chaplain and minister, I consider it a blessing to serve and address the physical, mental, and spiritual needs of others. Positive words, smiles, and lots of hugs offer hope and positively impact people's lives.

I will continue to strive to be extraordinary in God's eyes and fulfill my purpose because I desire the Lord to be pleased with my life. In this wonderful stage of adulthood, we are usually full of wisdom and have overcome a few bumps on the road of life. The experience and knowledge gained from our trials and tribulations, along with wonderful opportunities for friendship, commingling and communication, allow compassion to enter our hearts. We complain less and begin to understand and witness those who are clearly in a worse position or situation than anything we have complained about. Life has a way of teaching us valuable lessons when we witness and partake in these opportunities of learning. There are so many individuals in need of some form of help. It clearly takes a village. We all have a purpose, calling, and mission in life, let's give 110 percent because a little extra credit goes a long way. It can take us from ordinary to extraordinary!

—— ABOUT ——

Kristin Vaughan Robinson

Kristin Vaughan Robinson is a women's lifestyle editor, writer, and content strategist with more than twenty years of experience in media, print, and digital publishing fields. She began her career as a newspaper reporter at the *Philadelphia Inquirer* and *The Palm Beach Post* and later moved into the digital space, where she focused on women's lifestyle content, books, and entertainment. Her work has been published in *Essence, Black Enterprise*, Lifetime TV online, and the *Boston Globe*, as well as many other national publications. Kristin has held top editorial positions at digital properties, including Essence.com, Everyday Health, and Black Entertainment Television's website, BET.com, and has appeared as an on-air guest expert, red carpet contributor, speaker, and panelist. Kristin has regularly ghostwritten editorial content for some of the biggest names in women's health and fitness, including celebrity trainer Jillian Michaels, Denise Austin, and Joy Bauer and she is currently co-authoring several book projects. She is a graduate of Howard University and holds a master's degree from the University of Maryland. She lives in St. Albans, NY with her two children.

Emails:	kristin@kriscrossmedia.com
	kristinvaughan@outlook.com
Facebook:	Author Kristin Vaughan Robinson
Twitter:	@mskristinvr

ORDER MY STEPS

By Kristin Vaughan Robinson

"No. No! NO! NOOOO! NO..." I shook my head and screamed the word over and over again in disbelief. Like an echo, my voice faded from loud to soft until it trailed off and left my body limp on the bed.

It was Friday morning when I got "the call" from my father-in-law that Frank, my husband of nearly fifteen years, was in a car accident and he was never coming home from his Florida business trip. The love of my life, my best friend for more than two decades, and the father of our two beautiful children was gone. No goodbyes, just gone from our lives forever.

I remember that day in flashes of before and after moments. I took the kids to school that morning and told them Daddy would pick them up after school. I hurriedly packed my overnight bag for a quick trip to Washington D.C. with my college roommate to see then-President Barack Obama speak at my alma mater, Howard University. I had triumphantly pressed "send" on the final version of the first book in a children's series that I was co-authoring. I checked emails and felt giddy about *finally* getting a response to my press release from a magazine editor friend for my first client. I had been discouraged venturing out with my own writing and public relations business, but my biggest cheerleader, Frank, gave me a pep talk and sage advice two days earlier "to not be afraid to lean on my network"—and it worked.

I also remember that I uncharacteristically said to myself: "Thank you, God! I'm SO HAPPY right now!"—and meant it. At that moment, everything seemed better than great. After many years of uncertainty and anxiety, it felt like every aspect of my life was coming together all at once and I was excited! I grabbed my cell phone to text Frank my news, but I put it back down remembering that he was on the plane flying home to New York for Mothers' Day weekend—or so I thought.

He was already gone.

I dreaded the trip to school to pick up our babies, who were just six and nine years old at the time. I cursed every green traffic light that gave way for me to arrive at their school quickly that afternoon. Their questions came rapid fire: "Is Daddy in the car? I thought he was picking us up." "Are we going to the airport now to get him?" "Are you still going to see President Obama?" I mumbled incoherent half-truths to put off the inevitable. Back inside the walls of the home that Frank and I literally built together, I had no choice but to say the words that I never in a million years thought I would have to say to them. Their faces. Their cries. *Oh, their cries.* Their hearts literally breaking before my eyes…

More than a year later, nothing is what it was. None of us are who we once were. There were so many days, weeks, and months of disbelief. Truth be told, there still are. I watched our kids mature in front of my eyes that day and each day since. There are only traces of the "rainbows and unicorns" that Frank teased were constantly dancing around in our daughter's head. Their fears for safety—not theirs as much as mine—aren't what friends their ages typically worry about. Things like, "If Mommy leaves will she die too and will we become orphans?" When parents wave to us in the schoolyard, we aren't rushing to Ninja Warrior Training or robotics classes anymore, we're probably headed to one of our grief support groups. Their newest friends are "just like them;" kids who are also learning to cope with the loss of a parent or sibling before they even hit double-digits.

They've also regressed. My son's childlike behaviors returned and when he went back to school in September, those quick-tempered responses that we worked so hard to control came back too. My daughter obsessed over Mr. Snuggles, a massive teddy bear she took everywhere and propped in Daddy's chair in his office, or at the dinner table. Instead of their beds, they piled into my king-size bed where our epic popcorn-filled family movie nights were held. For months that first summer, our three bodies clung together, intertwined into a shared fetal position under a feather "dreamcatcher" on the right side of the bed that I still claim as "my side." We wrapped ourselves in each other's arms like a security blanket against the world. I didn't know if or how, we would or could, come out of this nightmare, but I knew it was too much for any of us to bear alone. The only way we would make it through was together, as a family. Early on, I made a rule: No one was going to go behind a closed bedroom door to cry, withdraw, or rage with anger alone. We were going to stay in Mommy and Daddy's bed and whether we were going to sob, scream, shout, hug, share, mourn, and eventually (hopefully) laugh and smile again, we would do it together.

But I wasn't ready for that yet. I was not ready to be without Frank. He was my soul mate, my confidant, my go-to for advice, my dance partner through life, my travel buddy, my fellow foodie, my love… He was a born Dad who was hands on. He did all the pickups and drop-offs when he wasn't traveling for business. He ruled with an open heart, generous hugs, and tons of laughs. The kids adored him, just like his many, many friends and colleagues all over the country did too. He was our world and we were his. Totally. Completely. Period. End. Full stop. Now he was gone.

We met through one of my best friends when we were just teenagers. I lived in Maryland. He lived in New York. Still, our friendship evolved and bloomed into a beautiful relationship, marriage, and family. He was the funniest person I knew. He was smart, the life of the party, and the person who made me feel sure that no matter what, everything was going to be all right. He wasn't perfect nor did we have the perfect marriage. We worked for what we had, but we were always clear that we were in it for the long haul and willing to pay our dues. We loved each other in a simple, effortless way, that didn't need flash and glitz—although sometimes we had that too—to endure. We kept a crazy, chaotic schedule that put our young family first, and was our blessed mess.

Frank and I were fully engulfed in our typical fast-paced life that Friday morning. We had plans. We had goals. We were RSVP'd for events, booked for our family vacation to Oak Bluffs on Martha's Vineyard and we were in the throes of planning our kids' May and June birthday celebrations. After that, there was Father's Day and Frank's forty-fifth birthday falling within the same week. Our fifteenth wedding anniversary was coming up in October. We were busy and in the middle of living.

This couldn't be real.

I was numb. I had stacks of daily affirmation books, journals, adult coloring books, and grief-themed books piled high. As a long-time journalist who was just embarking on pursuing my dream of authoring and co-writing books, I was now a writer who could not write, and an avid reader who could not read. My mind was scattered and my emotions were jumbled. Grief aside, I was exhausted; my anxiety and stress over how my family would survive financially, emotionally, and mentally were off the charts. The dreams and career goals that were finally falling in line with Frank's help, seemed now more like pipe dreams, never to be reimagined. I could no longer envision a "now" or a today, let alone a tomorrow, next week, or a future.

Then another series of losses, disappointments, and stresses hit our family one after another. The waves of grief and despair engulfed me. I was overwhelmed. I felt the pain so deeply I couldn't move. I couldn't pick myself up, *not one more time*. Frank prided himself in being a "chaos manager," but without him, everything spun out of control. I was lost in the current and too exhausted and heartbroken to fight it. I was relieved to just rest, even if it meant sinking or letting the undertow thrash me around and drag me further from the shore. I could feel the waves pulling me deeper into the abyss, waiting to swallow me whole.

I knew that if the darkness got its grips firmly on me that it would take more than I had to pull myself out of it. I thought of our kids. They were blessings and living testaments to our life and love. I had to be resilient and strong for them first, until I could be strong for myself. They had been through so much already. They needed me now more than ever; I *had* to show up. They deserved more than for me to become a shell of their mom, under the covers with the curtains drawn. It wasn't until I sunk to that lowest point, where I could barely make out the haze of light *way* at the top of the water's surface, that I finally tried to swim toward it—for them.

For months, I had turned myself inside out trying to make sense out of something that made no sense to me. I tried to find a way to accept that I would never get an answer or understand *WHY* God took Frank away from us. I struggled the most with making peace with that. What did God want from me? There is a saying, *there is a lesson and a blessing in everything.* What was the lesson and blessing in this one?

I decided to trust in the Lord. While I would never understand it while I was here on Earth, I believed there had to be something good that was to come out of all this pain. Happiness felt like a distant childhood memory that you know you'll never get a chance to relive, yet I couldn't help wanting it for me and our kids again. Somehow, I had to believe that our family was going to be okay. Somehow, we had to move forward and get back on track. Maybe in a different form and at a different time, but I had to believe that my life was divinely orchestrated through both the good and the bad times. God wasn't through with me yet.

Deep down in my soul, I knew that while my journey here with Frank was over; my individual journey was not. There were dreams planted deep inside of me and our children that had yet to come to fruition. But my future and plans had been expertly meshed with his since the days when we began talking seriously about marriage in my mid-twenties. It had been "we," not "me," for the last twenty years. Now, as the only remaining parent of two children, I had no clue what my purpose outside of parenting was—or how to find it.

I decided to step out on faith—which, at the time, was truly the size of the proverbial mustard seed. I forced myself to look for gratitude in everything throughout the day. I gave thanks for God's favor all day long. I surrounded myself with affirmations and set my day's intention each morning with three daily devotional books. I turned off tear-jerking, and violent television shows—especially the evening news—and limited my social media newsfeed. I listened to uplifting music and sermons on my satellite radio that planted seeds of hope, faith, and promise in my soul. I begged for mercy when other challenges and adversity arose, and praised the Lord when things calmed down again. I learned to be gentle with myself during this process and to remind myself that grieving has a different timeline for everyone. Still, I had no choice but to try to heal and give myself permission to search for a new joy and sense of peace.

I prayed for the Lord to "order my steps," like in the lyrics of my favorite gospel hymn by late African-American composer, Glenn Burleigh. The words moved me so much that I had insisted a soloist sing the song during Frank's home-going services. Unlike the other hymnals sung that day, it was included to give ME strength to move forward. It would become my rallying cry whenever I needed strength. *Order my steps in your Word, dear Lord / Lead me, guide me every day/ Send your anointing/ Father, I pray / Order my steps in your Word.*

I was completely overwhelmed and needed guidance. I swallowed my pride and learned to ask for and accept help, to manage all the household responsibilities that had fallen on me. Many of them were completely outside of my wheelhouse at the time. I wasn't equipped to handle the massive tasks that I now faced… alone. And, even if I could, there was no prize waiting for me for doing so.

A core team of amazing family and friends got in formation to help. They didn't just check in; they dove in. They researched, made calls, stood in lines, waded through the bureaucracy, encouraged me, even got me out of bed and dressed me. They hired help, problem-solved, babysat, and responded to my insomnia-fueled texts in the wee hours of the morning, and too many other things to list. Some even organized the kids' birthday parties in the days after the funeral, set up funds, fulfilled Frank's dream to send my daughter to Kennedy Space Center space camp, and planned a memorial golf tournament on his 46th birthday weekend.

I grew stronger as I made progress and chipped away at the mounds of paperwork and tasks. My learning curve was steep and I wore many new hats that had to be switched daily. I started to keep something I call a "Daily Congratulations" journal to give myself props when I accomplished something I didn't know how to do before. The Lord was ordering my steps.

I noticed that my children were always watching me when they thought I wasn't looking. They were taking cues from me. So, I made sure I got up and drove them to summer camp nearly every day whether I was in a funk or not. I often dropped them off at the entrance and as soon as they were out of sight I released the flood of tears I had been holding back the entire drive. Whether I was going back to bed or to my twice-weekly therapy sessions, I made sure to fix my face before I picked them up in the afternoon and tried to project optimism and positivity. While I had broken down several times in front of them—and I think children need to see parents grieving to know it's okay—I refused to be their burden. Eventually, I stopped crying every day. The tears still came in bursts, but less frequently.

We grew closer as a family. It felt safe sharing our feelings. We spoke Daddy's name often, laughed over funny memories, and remarked at the many loving signs he was sending us. We tuned into each other's frequencies and learned instinctively when we each needed a lift. My son made sure I had my "morning snuggle" and climbed in my bed like clockwork first thing each day. My daughter would simply walk up to me and put an arm on each shoulder and say, "If anyone can do it Mommy, you can." Then she'd walk away. Her encouragement often caused me to do a double take as if Frank had uttered the encouraging words himself. I wrapped them up in a bubble of love and even added a long-awaited playful puppy to our home who helped lift the heaviness and restore joy.

Going through a loss changes you. It changed me. I missed our life. I would still do anything to get it back. But I had to choose getting *better* over getting *bitter*. I had to find a way to let go of the unanswered questions and the feelings of unfairness so they wouldn't consume me. In the meantime and in between time, I adopted a new phrase from a friend whose husband had battled a serious illness: "I'm not okay now, but I will be."

There is power in speaking in expectancy.

That phrase helped me keep afloat and got us through the first year with all its "firsts." We made it. We survived. I woke up on Day One of Year Two, determined that this year we'll do more than survive, we'll thrive. Those business and co-writing book opportunities I was excited to work on "before" have started to present themselves again "after." I'm slowly veering my ship back on course and charting new directions in my life.

On our last Christmas together, for reasons that I don't even think he could grasp, Frank gave me a plaque that read, "God Knows When." He said that he "just had to buy it for me." I was confused, but he explained that I was always so worried and impatient about where my life and career were going and when they would get there. He bought it to remind me that "the timing in life isn't up to us. It's up to God."

Now, as I embark on this unchartered road, that plaque serves as a daily reminder from him to stay on a path of faith. That although my life may not make sense to me, I do believe that my steps are divinely ordered. Every day is a new day taken one step at a time. I don't know what's next for us, but I do know in my heart that whether we are "okay" now or not, by the grace of God, and on the strength of Frank's love, one day we will be.

———— ABOUT ————

Sony JM Thornton

Sony JM Thornton is a professional life and career coach. She specializes in personal and professional development, for woman to create success that is balanced, with an emphasis on life transition and to reach their greatest in life from career advancement, to transitioning from the workplace to entrepreneurship. She seeks to aid in life transitions, including helping working mothers and any woman in search of work-life balance, to help them find their true passion and joy.

In addition to being a professional life coach, Thornton is also an advocate for domestic violence survivors and advocates against sex trafficking. Her passion is to help promote self-happiness and to rebuild self-esteem and self-love in women who have experienced broken moments and need a plan of action for a new beginning, or to reignite the joy that already exists within.

With over twenty years as a Human Resources professional, specializing in executive and leadership development, coaching, employee relations, conflict and compassion resolution including mediation, she has acquired the knowledge and leadership skills to work effectively with people from all walks of life. Her wide range of experiences includes balancing a career in Corporate America and in nonprofit, which empowers her to assist others find their path to success and a joyful life.

What makes Thornton different is her level of integrity, passion, and a warm spirit that encourages others to see their own great potential and to reach for joy in life. She makes a difference in people's lives while empowering women to achieve bountiful success and happiness.

Email:	sonylifecoach@aol.com
Twitter:	sonylifecoach
LinkedIn:	sony-jm-thornton-lifecoach
Facebook:	Simply-joy-108993579772563/
Tumblr:	simplyjoynow

STRENGTH FROM BEYOND, NEVER DENIED

By Sony JM Thornton

By waiting and by calm you shall be saved,
In quiet and in trust your strength lies.

— Isaiah 30:15

Even as child I had a knack for helping others and was the spokesperson for my then recently immigrated family in Brooklyn, New York. I arrived in the United States from Haiti in March of 1979 at the age of seven years old, speaking only French and Haitian Creole languages and was placed in all English speaking elementary classes. In less than six months, from what I remember, I went from not speaking any English to speaking English like it was my native language. Besides, my uncle, I was the only English speaking child. What that means to Haitian immigrant families is that you are the designated Family Press Secretary. This is not a job you can turn down or be fired from. My Grandmother and my mother elected me to translate letters, applications and serve as the translator for as many family and friends of the family, as they could find. By the time I held a real job, I had navigated through so much paperwork and difficult conversations and problems in my younger age, that most of my adult work challenges were not very difficult. I helped as many people as I could, and when I was weary, as most kids get, my Grandmother and mother would hug me, praise me, and encourage me to do the best I could. My Grandmother always said, "If you are going to help someone, do it with all your heart."

This was the start of my Grandmother sealing her words of wisdom into my soul. I was in awe of her; Grandmother Lilia Sylvestre, was love, joy, and peace to me. She shared so many sensible sayings that have resonated with me, and now I see, that for as long as I have known her, she has been preparing me to survive in this world. When I was faced with challenges and feeling stressed and worried, Grandmother would say, "pray to God baby." When I prayed and things did not change the next day, I would share my worries with her and she would gently pull me closer and say, "You can't pray to God and worry at the same time. If you trust in God, you have to truly believe that he will work it out for you." She didn't believe that God would do it all, she just did *not* believe that you needed to sit and worry if you prayed. She would say to me, "pray and let it go." It became my motto, but at times I really struggled with this belief. She would tell me that, "I see great things in you and what God has given you no one else can take from you." She constantly reminded me of the strength that God has placed within me no matter what adversities or challenges I faced. As a child, Grandmother made me feel that I had amazing abilities and was special. That feeling has stayed with me. When I was a little girl, Grandmother often told me, that she won't always be here on earth with me and I should listen and take note because one day, when she is gone, I will remember the things she has told me. She said this so often it became just another saying that we hear our grandparents, parents, and our loved ones say to us over and over again, that we truly don't understand the meaning until much later in life. Little did I know that Grandmother's words would later save me and provide guidance to enable me to continue to help others.

In 2008 and 2009, my world was slowly falling apart. In early 2008, both my Grandmother and my father-in-law became very ill. During, this time, my father started to show signs that he was also sick with degeneration of the spine. My mother was disabled at home from a car accident a few year's prior that nearly killed her and my father. From June 2008 to the end of that year, my father-in-law passed, my Grandmother's heart condition got progressively worse, and my father had surgery for spine degeneration. I was working full time in a very demanding human resources position, and I was a full-time Mom, to my beautiful teen daughter, with no support from my then estranged and now ex-husband. My body was so exhausted that I had all kinds of anxiety, but I continued to help my family, anyone at work and at home, and be there for my friends. I often cried myself to sleep, but most nights, I didn't have the strength to cry, and I was so scared that this heavy load of responsibility was slowly suffocating me. I felt like I couldn't breathe. But no one ever saw that side of me. I was not in a loving relationship that nurtured my heart with companionship and love. It was all work, and family, or all family and work. I was seriously drained and losing my grip on life. My faith, soul, and heart were in despair and I was simply going through the motions of life and not really living.

In the mornings, on my drive to work, I would call Grandmother and talk with her during the couple of hours of morning traffic, another thing that made be crazy. During this time she would feed my soul and heart. It felt like she was breathing life back into my lungs. She was the one who helped me hold things together and remind me that joy already lived within me. Now when I think of it, she was my anchor while I was anchoring everyone else. She reminded me that God would give me strength, and protect me and would always guide me. She'd say, "Although God will be there for you, you have to take care of yourself too. Make time for happiness, quiet time and for praying." She would insist, that my kind heart does not mean I have to do it all because everyone is relying on me. She would encourage me to ask my siblings, who were all still younger than me, to step up. I promised her that I would take care of myself more, but she knew me better and she would say "then let me see you let go of some of this load."

I was so grateful for our talks and I would be rejuvenated for the day. Then the cycle of my life would continue and I was again busy attending to family and work, and not myself. My morning conversations with Grandma, which we've had for many years, are particularly important to me now. They are my healing grace and they refresh my spirit. Her ability to sooth my innermost anxiety with her prayers and her majestic words—that surely angels had given her or Jesus himself—never ceased to comfort me. I know she prayed for me because she said so and I know she loved me wholeheartedly because she not only said it, she showed me by delivering her messages directly to the depth of my heart and spirit. To remind me of God's love and words; she would repeat Proverbs 3-5:6: *Trust in the Lord with all your heart and lean not on your own understanding; in all your ways submit to him, and he will make your paths straight.* I later discovered that she shared this grace with anyone who needed it. I would never be finished hearing Grandmother's words and the amazing ways she shows her love and shared the peace that God gave her. She told me that God's peace was within me and he will always be with me, and I should not worry about so much. I would feel filled with her words, but life continued to overwhelm me and for many years I suffered silently.

Then on August 15th, 2009, my uncle called me very early in the morning to share the news of my Grandmother's passing, and for a moment I couldn't breathe again. My breath stopped and I felt my heart close to breaking. I was numb, dizzy, scared; and I felt completely alone as I sat in my room in a two-family house that was filled with family. I must have cried because he said, "It's okay, she's not suffering anymore." Then he sadly whispered in disbelief, "My mom is really gone." We both cried softly.

I still couldn't breathe but I knew this time, I could not call Grandmother for her to bring comfort into my aching heart. Her words would no longer give me life again. I went outside on the porch and sat on the steps. I looked at the garden and remembered that only a few weeks ago, Grandmother was on this very porch watching me cut daffodils to place in a vase that I would bring to her room. And now she is gone. As I wrapped my arms around myself, I felt a very soft and warm spirit caressing me, it could have been the cool morning air, but I choose to believe it was Grandmother's spirit. I exhaled deeply, breathed in fully and let out another breath. Then I cried uncontrollably on the porch.

My sister and daughter were inside sleeping in their rooms and I did not have the heart to share the news of Grandma's passing but I would have to do it very soon. I needed some time to be alone with my broken heart and to pray. I wanted to talk with Grandma and for the first time in my life, I looked at the sky, I felt really small in this great big world. I felt my anxiety rising, and I started to tremble and shake as I tried to find ways to comfort my empty soul. It was then in that moment I discovered the joy of surrendering to God and I prayed for him to give me peace and to fill me up with his comfort and love. Then I remembered Isaiah 30:15, *By waiting and by calm you shall be saved, in quiet and in trust your strength lies.*

Then of course, I went straight into busy mode. I ran around so much preparing for her funeral and supporting my mother and the family, that I did not see or predict the train wreck I was about to become. I was consumed with planning and making sure I honored Grandmother's wishes for her home-going services. She had entrusted her final wishes to me because she knew I would carry them out exactly as she wanted.

We had a beautiful day for Grandma's funeral, but along with the beauty that day held, I remember the heart-wrenching pain of the loss of my Grandmother. As I sat again on the porch I realized that I was beyond broken. I looked up at the sky and the magnitude of losing Lilia Sylvestre, my Grandmother, hit me like a car crashing through by body to my soul. As I looked up into the sky and took in its glory, my eyes became fixed on clouds that resembled angel's wings. I felt a stab of pain through my chest as I now fully comprehended the fact that Grandma was no longer here with me. I curled up in the chair into a fetal position and I screamed and cried like I was fighting for my life.

I was in shock and disbelief as I realized that I could no longer call my Grandmother on the phone, or take her shopping. I could no longer buy her pretty dresses, or give her Mother's Day cards, gifts, or flowers. I could no longer enjoy her favorite holidays with her. I would no longer have my favorite Haitian food that only she could make. I could no longer celebrate her birthdays with her, hug and kiss her, or bring her daffodils cut from our garden for her room. Most of all, I could no longer hear her loving and comforting voice or her words of wisdom and love. I was devastated, paralyzed with grief as I finally understood what Grandmother's death truly meant. My eyes swelled again with tears that ran down my face and felt like fire. The wrenching pain in my heart was unbearable and I knew that I had never known pain like this. There was a hole in my heart and in my life that will never be filled. No one could replace my Grandmother. I opened my mouth to scream to God "why?" but there was no sound. There was only agony in my soul.

For years Grandma would tell me, "I won't always be here and when I'm gone you'll miss me." She was right. I truly missed her and I didn't know how I would make it without her. I thought my spirit would forever be broken and my heart will never be healed. Even as I grieved I still had to deal with life's burdens. I was anxious and scared, but no one saw that I was slipping into emotional quicksand because I tried not to let it show. But I was quietly losing my mind. I went to therapy for my brokenness and fear, but that was not enough. My emptiness was beyond the medical profession. I had no choice but to turn to what gave Grandma strength, peace, and endless joy—God. I would repeat prayers of peace and love every day and one of my Grandmother's favorite bible prayers, Isaiah 26: 1-9, became my own. I would say it almost daily while my heart was grieving. *Peace I leave you; my peace I give you. I do not give to you as the world gives. Do not let your hearts be troubled and do not be afraid.* My prayers helped me take baby steps toward healing and feeling like joy was filling my heart again.

Somehow with God giving me strength I've found my way. The warmth, love and prayers that my Grandmother shared with me, became my pillar of comfort and has inspired me to continue to share a relationship with God, the son and the Holy Spirit. Now I share her wisdom in all that I do. I hear her words flowing through me when I help family and friends. I even hear them at work. The graceful way she taught me to find my inner joy is still with me. Although I miss my Grandmother dearly; I can connect with her through the seeds of her spiritual teachings she has planted in me. It has laid the foundation for me to find creative ways to resolve my problems. Mornings can still be challenging for me but when I wake I pray: "Lord, I praise you and thank you for this day; I pray that your grace will guide my heart and my steps today and every day." I am now more spiritually centered. Prayer is at the core my life and I now very much appreciate quiet and downtime. I find ways to breathe and to be more flexible with life, and the many curves and detours that it brings don't scare me so much. I have moved own with my life and married a wonderful man who has shown me incredible love. My daughter has graduated from college and is starting her life, and my family strives to be more self-sufficient. I have made significant progress in letting my siblings do more. My hectic work environment remains, but I am waiting on God to lead me on a different path while he uses me as an instrument to help others. By waiting and by calm I became stronger and more spiritually grounded. I know Grandma can see me from beyond, and sees her strength within me and she is very proud indeed.

Grandma would tell me, that when she leaves this earth, she wants us all to have a happy life while remembering her and not waste time grieving for her. On the day of her funeral, that afternoon there was a beautiful rainbow over our house that lasted for a long time. I believe it was Grandma showering us with love and showing her presence from beyond. Oprah Winfrey and Maya Angelou have talked about how their Grandmothers changed the course of their lives, and now I understand what that kind of love can do to your mind, heart, and soul. That kind of love lasts a lifetime even if they are not with you. As my Grandmother told me, no matter what delays your journey to joy, God's love for you will never be denied. Now I feel her strength within me from beyond this earth, just as I feel the power of God's love and joy in me. I am so grateful for this amazing grace.

——— ABOUT ———
Dr. LaWana Firyali Richmond

Dr. LaWana Firyali Richmond is a Business Development Manager in the Transportation, Parking, and People Movement Department at University of California (UC) San Diego. Her responsibilities include project management, business analysis, customer and vendor relations, as well as change management. LaWana is a certified Project Management Professional with degrees in Marketing, Operations, Information Systems, and Educational Leadership.

Over the past twenty years, LaWana has been actively involved in community service and social justice endeavors. She is one of two inaugural Chrispeels Fellowship recipients and earned a doctorate in Educational Leadership from California State University, San Marcos, and the University of California, San Diego. Her research interests include leadership development and employee engagement as well as access to, and persistence in education.

LaWana is a member of the Advisory Board for the C. Montgomery Technology Fund, which supports community access to technology at the Malcolm X Library in southeast San Diego. She has served on the Executive Board of the African American Alumni Chapter of the San Diego State University Alumni Association, Executive Board of the UJIMA Network, Advisory Board of N.U.M.E.R.A.L.S. (formerly known as the Hadassah Project), Area 17 Governor for Western Division, District 5 of Toastmasters International, Chair of UC San Diego Black Staff Association, Chair-Elect and Chair of the UC San Diego Staff Association, as well as Junior and Senior Delegate for the Council of University of California Staff Associations.

Twitter:	firyvisions
	firyali
Facebook:	lawana.richmond
Email:	info@firyali.com
Website:	firyali.com

LOST AND FOUND

By Dr. LaWana Firyali Richmond

This story is less dramatic than many of the other significant moments in my life. It is however a moment when I learned something that serves me to this day.

I was a young mother with very little preparation for the life I had chosen. When it came to domestic leanings, I scoffed at many opportunities to learn, in favor of intellectual or hedonistic pursuits. When I didn't have my nose buried in a book, I wanted to party like it was 1999. That was an actual thing back then. My two favorite pastimes left little room for much else.

When I made the decision to be a mom, I knew I would have to make some changes, I just didn't know how true that was. Imagine going from being only loosely responsible for yourself because the adults in your life provided for you, to suddenly being responsible not only for yourself, but also a baby who looked to you for everything. Looking back, I realize I programmed my daughter to be independent and self-sufficient. She started early down that path and has stayed the course supporting herself from the day she left for college until today. Despite being born to an inexperienced and clueless young woman, she turned out okay. In case it's not already evident, please know I am very proud of her and the path she has chosen. Most importantly, know that she is okay; despite you what you heard next, don't be alarmed. It all turned out okay, in the end.

On the day in question, I was doing one of the most universally hated chores on the planet; washing clothes. Before I figured out it was unsustainable, I would buy new clothes to avoid doing laundry. It was a bright and sunny day, so I carried the baby, laundry, and the baby's tricycle down the stairs and to the laundry room near my apartment.

I was nineteen and the baby was three. Having reached the mature age of nineteen, I felt I had "adulting" down to a science. I knew what needed to be done and I knew how to do it. Or so I thought. Essentially, I didn't like being told what to do because I was a grown @ss woman. These particular bits of information are critical for context. One more important fact. When I moved out on my own, my new apartment was literally down the hill from my family home. I was close enough for my little brother to drop in to spot check and make sure I was okay. I remember how aggravated I used to get when he'd go into my kitchen and checked how much food I had on hand. In retrospect, I am grateful I had people who cared, but that is a learned response.

Being told I had ruined my life and that my poor child would never amount to anything was reverse psychology that added to my drive and determination to be and do more, not only for myself, but more importantly for my child. Again, I digress.

While doing laundry, I let my baby girl ride her tricycle behind me. I could hear her playing and laughing so I felt comfortable shifting my attention to the task at hand. I wanted to hurry and get the laundry done so we could go do something fun. I can't remember what that was, but it doesn't really matter anymore.

I was washing three loads of my clothes, her clothes and our linens. Whites, colors, and hot for towels and blankets were the only things running through my mind for a few minutes as I loaded the machines. Just as I closed the lid on the last load, I realized I didn't hear my daughter's squeaky tricycle wheel turning behind me.

I tried to not panic, but I could feel the tightening of my gut and little droplets of sweat on my upper lip. I rushed out of the laundry room hoping to see her nearby while simultaneously wrestling with the fear that she wasn't.

When I didn't see her, I still didn't go into full on panic. I felt like her trike would still be there if something bad had happened. At least that's what I kept telling myself. After exploring the areas near our apartment, I assured myself she must have ridden to the playground at the other end of the walkway. I ran to the playground expecting to see her tricycle abandoned as she played on the swings or the merry-go-round. She wasn't there. Next stop was the jungle gym.... Not there either. My little Jazz Renee' was nowhere to be found.

Panic rose inside me, but I refused to give in to my fears. Mind you, this was in the mid 1980's, so it was a different world. Much of what we see nowadays, on cable or news or find in our social media feeds and email inboxes, was not in wide distribution. If that had been the case I would've have been a lot more afraid for her.

Sadly, I was more afraid of my mom. Remember, she was just up the hill. Luckily, I was in the neighborhood I "grew up" in (realizing in retrospect that I was not yet grown at the time). I knew lots of the local teens and young adults. I managed to round up a group of about ten people to help me search the neighborhood for my child. The one caveat was, "Please don't tell my mom..."

Where I lived at the time was a low income apartment complex in Clairemont, which means nothing if you're not from San Diego, but people used to call it Squaremont. It was kinda suburban. We knew people in apartments and houses all over the neighborhood. Growing up we used to take turns hanging out and having slumber parties at each other's homes. We were a relatively close-knit community. The upside was how easy it was to find people to help me look. The downside was everybody was in everybody else's business. How could we conduct a "wide scale" search without alerting my mom, or one of her friends who would then tell her?

After a couple of hours, the sun started to go down and I realized I had no choice. It was time to bring in the big guns. I was so full of shame and fear as I approached my mother's door. My heart was heavy as I lifted my hand to knock.

I must've made a lot of noise during my approach. Maybe I was dragging my feet. I have no idea, but before I could knock, the door opened and I was face to face with my mother. Now my mom is not a violent person, nor is she much of a yeller or a screamer. It was her look of disappointment I was trying to avoid.

My mother is an amazing woman. Soon after my parents parted ways, my brother and I were on a plane with our mother to start a new life in California. She was still a young woman with urges and leanings of her own, but she put us first. Our mother moved to San Diego and made a life not only for herself but also for her children. She didn't start out with much, but we never felt deprived. She took excellent care of us. I never pretended to think I could live up to her example, but I was loathe to disappoint her any more than I already had.

In case you haven't figured it out already, I love my mother. So much of who I am is because of what I learned, not just from what she said, but more from what she did. She introduced me to art, poetry, science fiction, and history long before the San Diego Unified School District even made its first attempt. She is still, hands down, the best cook I've ever known and remains a beauty to behold. When I look at her I feel a surge of hope that her genetic legacy will kick in and I'll be looking as good as she does well into my twilight years.

This story is hard to tell, not because of the outcome but because of my shame. I was doubly shamed on this day. The first part of my shame was losing track of a three year old on a tricycle. In and of itself, that was enough. The second part of my shame was the way I responded when I realized I had a problem. I tried to hide my problem and thereby increased my shame.

My mother opened the door just as I was taking a deep breath to prepare myself for what was to come. I knew I had messed up and not only had I messed up, I had failed to find my own solution. I had gone to my mother looking for her help. I knew I needed it, but I also knew the shame and humiliation I imagined would come with it, and I wanted none of that.

My mother was the first to break the silence. I can only guess at how I must have looked to her. I'm certain I was disheveled and the expression on my face must've filled in some of the blanks. She knew I hadn't been out goofing around. Something had happened. She asked me what was wrong.

Just then, I heard a familiar squeak, and over my mother's shoulder I saw my daughter riding her tricycle around the living room. It was too late to hold back the tears, but I was so relieved. I tried to hide my distress, but I couldn't hide anything from her then any more than I can now.

When I laid out the whole sorry series of events, she laughed at me. She laughed long and hard as I sat there, dumbfounded. At first my feelings were a little hurt, and then I laughed with her. I laughed at the ridiculousness of my thought process. I had spent all that time having everyone tiptoe around when I should've just gone to her in the first place.

My daughter had become bored with going back and forth on the same little patch of area I had directed her to stay in while I loaded the washers. She took it upon herself to ride her tricycle up the hill to my mother's house. She then walked up the stairs and knocked on the door. Someone carried the trike up for her and she was content. She'd been there the whole time.

This brings me to my second shameful act of the day. Probably more of an inaction. A lot of my heartache and stress would've been avoided if I had just gone to my mom's in the first place. The big lesson I learned that day was to ask for help when I needed it. That seems simple enough and on the surface I did ask for help, but I didn't ask for the right help. I knew my mom was amazing and even if my daughter hadn't been there, she would have helped me through that storm. My almost fifty-year-old self can see that very clearly. The nineteen year old was not so wise.

Quite often, we do that in life. We either fail to ask for help or go looking for it in all the wrong places. How many times have you avoided admitting to a mistake or mishap or didn't ask for help because of the potential "I told you so" you imagined was waiting in the wings? What's the big deal about hearing, "I told you so"? The only thing that comes up for me is wounded pride. Some might call it a feeling of humiliation.

When I was shopping for my first car, a friend helped me look. Being a young adult, I wanted something "fly." I wanted to not only get to my destination but also look good in the process. My friend shared with me something her father told her when she was in a similar position. "A humble ride will take you much farther than a proud walk." After mulling that over for a few moments, I promptly purchased the humble ride that had been presented for my consideration. I must say, that humble ride served me well. The use of the words humble and proud in a sentence were the perfect triggers to get me to reassess my thinking.

The moment I realized I could have "found" my daughter much earlier if I had been able to humble myself and ask my mother for help has stayed with me. The delay in this case was not long. The only thing blocking my blessing was me. I could've moved out of my own way much sooner and avoided a lot of anguish. When I'm afraid to ask for help or speak truth to power, I am taken back to that day. The way I felt in that moment, is at the heart of every time I seem fearless.

I learned the harm of not facing my fears. I learned the strength that comes every time I realize it is never as bad as I was afraid it would be. This knowledge has become a driving force in my life. When I consider trying something new or taking any kind of risk, I remind myself to not let fear guide or rule my life. I do not claim—nor ever wish—to be fearless. Fear is not our enemy. It alerts us to be cautious or thoughtful about the next steps. At the same time, things are almost never as bad as we are afraid they might be.

With that driving force, I have raised two children, completed four college degrees, spoken before groups large and small, as well as advocated for, and provided leadership to my peers and many people from various socioeconomic communities. Today, I am not fearless. I am just willing to face those fears as I continue to push forward and make my way through life.

---- ABOUT ----

Deneen Cooper

Deneen Cooper is the President of Uplift and Impact Career Counseling LLC founded in 2011. Its mission is: To uplift and impact the lives of individuals by acknowledging strengths and limiting weaknesses. Being in the field of Human Resources for twenty-six years working for some of the largest organizations in the world enabled her to understand the reasons companies make the hiring decisions they do. After surviving breast cancer and becoming disabled with spinal disease, Deneen realized it was her divine mission and gift to counsel people with valuable career information. Living with serious health challenges gives a perspective on GOD'S calling on you. Life is too short to waste your GOD-given gifts and not live in your purpose.

The heart of a man plans his way but the Lord establishes his steps.— Proverbs 16:9

She is now embarking on a long time desire to be an author. Deneen is single and has lived in the Bronx for fifty-three years. She is the daughter to her eighty-four year old father and sister to her two brothers. A University of North Carolina alum who bleeds Carolina Blue and White.

GO TARHEELS!!!

Phone:	917-747-1994
Email:	deneenblessed@aol.com
	dcblessed@outlook.com
Facebook:	Deneen Cooper
Twitter:	@upliftimpact
Instagram:	deneenblessed
LinkedIn:	deneenuplift

DISABLED BUT NOT DERAILED

By Deneen Cooper

I know for sure my challenges pushed me into GOD'S vision for my life. Living in your purpose sometimes comes out of your greatest pain. My business, Uplift and Impact Career Counseling was created after twenty-five years of working in human resources. My disability took me out of the corporate craziness that I probably wouldn't have left on my own.

As an HR professional, when I interviewed candidates for various positions, it turned into counseling sessions. I shared the nuances about what my colleagues and I looked for when hiring. Now I am able to open doors and have life-changing intimate connections with people during one of the most anxious decision-making times in their life, choosing a career path. Serving and helping people to navigate the next steps in their career brings me the greatest joy. As my mantra states, "to uplift and impact the lives of individuals by highlighting their strengths and limiting their weaknesses."

Reflecting on my life, 2013 was a very rough year. I endured a breast lumpectomy along with seven weeks of radiation therapy and cancer didn't win! Just as I was rebounding from that ordeal, I was sent to the hospital for an emergency artery embolization to stop hemorrhaging from uterine fibroids. My gynecologist said I was a walking heart attack waiting to happen. I've always thought of myself as a resilient woman but this was a lot, even for me. I was a walking testimony to the scripture, *No weapon formed against me shall prosper.*

As I bounced back from all of this illness, I found myself the happiest I had ever been. I was recently engaged during Christmas in 2012 to Ellis, an unbelievable man I had met on a dating website. He was everything I had prayed for and we were building our lives together. There had always been an emptiness in my spirit since my mom had passed. She would've been with me through every phase of this health journey but my family, close sister-friends and Ellis made it endurable. As I focused my energies back on work and my relationship, something, which I couldn't put my finger on, just didn't seem right. A nudging on my spirit that kept saying, "What doesn't kill you, will make you stronger."

I was so happy that we were able to take our biannual trip to Vegas at the end of 2013 and 2014 was off to a great start. I resumed my bimonthly weekend trips to Atlantic City to see Ellis and he was back and forth visiting me in the Bronx. Even though the illness had taken a toll on some aspects of our relationship, I was getting my mojo back. When I was initially diagnosed with cancer, I told Ellis that we should break up. I didn't know where this journey was going to take me and he hadn't signed up for the uncertainty. The man I fell in love with assured me that no matter what happened, he would always be there for me. A big part of me believed him but I knew a shift was about to happen. GOD was going to test me in ways that I couldn't even imagine and I had spoken some things into existence.

When your body looks different and your energy levels decrease tremendously, everything changes. Did I blame Ellis for looking elsewhere for what I couldn't provide? Of course I did, but in reality I wasn't the same woman. The illnesses had changed me not just physically but also mentally. My get up and go truly got up and went. I was angry at him for not being honest but I was angrier at myself because the handwriting was on the wall. It took some really truthful conversations, prayer, and forgiveness from both of us to get past the hurt. There's a great quote I follow as it relates to forgiving. "Forgiveness is giving up the hope that the past could have been any different." What remained after all that hurt was a lasting friendship and I was going to need it now more than ever.

I fell twice in one week. What the heck was happening to me? The fall outside of my apartment building really scared me. This just wasn't me tripping over my feet; something else was happening. My primary physician referred me for physical therapy and I was being treated for tightness in my back. After months of physical therapy things weren't getting any better. While all this was happening, I made the decision to leave my consultant gig. It was mentally taxing and I was having problems getting to meetings because I had difficulty walking. It was gradual, but walking NYC streets will let you know quick fast and in a hurry if something isn't right. I was getting frustrated with the doctors and physical therapists because I knew it was more than a back issue.

Finally, I picked an orthopedic doctor because her name looked friendly and she was local. As soon as she saw me walk, she sent me to a neurologist. After a whole year of being misdiagnosed, the neurologist finally gave me the verdict. Degenerative Spondylislothesis of the cervical and lumbar spine. The name itself sent me into a teary mess because I knew it was serious. Although I was relieved to know what was wrong with me, I was also scared to death. How could I have spinal disease? I'd never experienced a traumatic event or played a sport and just couldn't grasp that my spine was deteriorating. When I sat with my orthopedic surgeon who told me that my cervical spine had three areas of deterioration and if I didn't have surgery immediately, I would be paralyzed. I had only 30 percent movement in my legs and the surgery would get me to at least 50 percent but I would never be at 100 percent. I was devastated. Fifty-one years old and I am disabled. I survived cancer, this couldn't be happening.

The person I thought about most was my Daddy. He was eighty-two years old, widowed, retired and now he'd have to help take care of his disabled daughter. Thank GOD I'd always lived with my parents but how were we going to manage? I wanted to have a pity party and sit in my depression, but I put on my big girl panties and did all the research I could on the disease. When I had cervical spinal surgery on January 15, 2016, I knew I was going to be all right. Once my cervical spine was fused and healed, I now had to focus on my lumbar spine, which was also starting to deteriorate.

Through all of this, my biological and my heavenly Father have been my strength. My Daddy, a quiet and supportive man, showed up in ways that I couldn't even imagine. His baby girl was going through some things and I needed him and my brothers. I knew they loved me but sometimes it takes a life-changing event to show you just how much.

My heavenly Father is another story. I always knew GOD and believed in salvation but this journey strengthened my relationship because at my lowest, *all I had* was GOD. My resolve and love for life is not taken for granted because I know that life can change in an instant. I'm a living and breathing testimony. For what was taken from me, I received so much back. My family connection is now stronger than ever. My circle of sister-friends became smaller because this journey is not for the faint of heart. Ellis, my ex-fiancé is still one of my closest friends.

Although there may be tough days ahead, my destiny will not be determined by my disability. My story is made up of many peaks and valleys. The great thing about being in a valley is that there is no other way to go, but up. There is a quote that tells me there is a reason for all of this. "Never be ashamed of what you've been through as GOD will use your story for his GLORY." I'm disabled but not derailed. My blessings may be delayed but never denied.

ABOUT

Theresa Adair

Theresa Adair is a native of St. Louis, MO and currently lives in San Diego, CA. She is a career woman, a life and fitness coach, an entrepreneur; an influential leader, a motivational speaker, and a person who hopes to inspire others to be the best versions of themselves.

Theresa has framed her career in innovating to help society, delighting in community, and exalting beauty in patterns and invention. She has worked for a telecommunication company for more than fifteen years and she also a US Navy Reserve Intelligence Officer. As a life and fitness coach, she has helped people to evolve, empower, and express themselves in their own authentic way.

She also serves on the board of directors for organizations that promotes Science, Technology, Engineer, and Mathematics (STEM) to the youth, especially girls and women, by teaching them how to code.

She is a game changer, powerful, fearless and selfless. Making a difference is her passion.

Instagram:	flawless45adair
Website:	iamtheresaadair.com
Email:	info@iamtheresaadair.com
Facebook:	iamtheresaadair

MY JOURNEY TO SELF-CARE AND SELF LOVE

By Theresa Adair

Behind my "S" was a woman who was considered as a Super mom, a Superwoman, a Strong women and a Super wife. But the "S' on my chest was really meant for being stressed and suicidal. The battle for self-care and self-love has taken years; it is an ongoing battle.

My earliest memory of depression was my first year after college. It was about ten years later before I realize I was depressed but, up until that point, I don't think I would have known how to identify depression. Our society emphasizes the belief that women, especially black women, are inherently strong. Don't get me wrong, we definitely are, but the problem with this belief has to do with the assumption that we are supposed to *always* be strong. The pressure to consistently be the source of strength for everyone but yourself is a heavy load.

Being strong is a very stressful burden that I've carried silently for most of my life. Growing up I was surrounded by strong black women and men, but there was something about the women that fueled my aspirations. I saw women who were independent and who were defiant about not being what society says a woman has to be. My mother and Grandmother are examples of the strongest women I know. Watching them, I learned they were not emotional women unless angered. There were only a few occasions when I saw my mother cry. I desired her strength and ability to suppress pain. People always go to my mother for help and she was always a wonderful example of a strong woman. However, I'm sure at times that strength must have felt like a burden. Especially when my Grandmother passed. I remember my mother taking care of others while also making all the funeral arrangements. Though she cried a few times during the process, those tears that streamed down her face showed strength.

For years I was a consummate workaholic, while at the same time being a wife and mother of two children. I also maintained two jobs in industries where I was, for many years, the only woman. In addition to all that, I went to graduate school during that time. I was often called on to offer financial help to family members in need and was driven to over-commitment. I even stepped in to chair a nonprofit organization that promoted women of color in technology, which is a passion. As a matter of fact, I am one of the 15 percent of African American women in technology. At that time I was perceived as capable and competent to hold two jobs, one as a US. Navy Reserve Military officer and the other as a System Engineer at a telecommunication company. I was able to "rise above it all." And became the person that everyone turned to in order "to get things done."

I pride myself on suppressing my own hurts or needs and staying focused. I trained myself to not have to rely on others, and to take care of others instead. Which frequently meant putting myself last. An enormous amount of energy went into "appearing strong" when down inside I felt overwhelmed and sad. People called me "The Strong One." They would say that I would "Never let my guard down; always wore my game face." Occasionally, a flash of doubt or fear or anger erupted inside me under the weight of it all. At those times, I stayed busy. I believed that it was the price I paid for being a mother, wife, sister, daughter, co-worker, and so much more.

By 2008 I could no longer deal with it all. I was dying inside and masking it was killing me. My body could no longer take the stress. I was physically and emotionally broken. I felt like I was in a deep black hole that I was unable to climb out of. I was overwhelmed by all my responsibilities. I was building a name for myself as a Navy Reserve Intelligence Officer, which is a title that is held by less than 5 percent African American women and I was proud of my accomplishments. But I was also having marital issues. Coupled with the fact that I was taking care of my mother, and I had two teenagers who needed my attention. During this period, I was struggling daily to get out of bed, to eat, to sleep. There were days when I felt like even breathing was an impossible task, and sometimes I wondered if things would be easier if I just stopped breathing. My husband later noticed that I was becoming increasing distracted and had a hard time focusing on things. Of course I denied it. I finally realized, this time, I wasn't strong enough. I needed help. So I fought my way out of bed and onto a therapist's couch. I was exhausted carrying all the weight of life on my shoulders. But I knew that if I didn't get help quickly, I would not survive it.

People silently struggle with depression because they're afraid to speak up. The social stigma of mental illness affected my journey with depression as well. Thankfully, I got over that debilitating fear.

I had to sit with myself and ask some hard questions. I had to ask myself, what made my life meaningful. Overcoming was a daily struggle. Many days I found myself doing my best to survive, and while some of those days I may not have been 100 percent sure that surviving is what I truly even desired. To battle against these challenges I faced regarding both my physical and mental health, I followed these actions:

Self-Love

Make self-love a priority. Love yourself enough to fight for yourself. Self-love is the process of intentionally directing energy toward your advancement. It is not natural, but cultivated through labor. When you're defining your ideal life, you should ensure that you're not dismissing your personal goals and dreams for the sake of advancing other people's goals and dreams. There's a way to meet the expectations and demands of your home life and still give yourself permission to pursue your own selfish endeavors.

Practice Self-Care

Self-care is critical to living successfully with depression or any chronic illness. Life is inherently going to include pain and suffering that we must be committed to releasing. We have to eliminate every belief that supports the idea that strength is being emotionally blocked. Be resilient. Resilience means facing life's difficulties with courage and patience and refusing to give up. Our resilience should not be defined by our ability to withstand an immense amount of pain and suffering without breaking. Positive self-respect is the ability to open yourself up and experience your feelings while exchanging with others in an enriching way. I've developed the habit of focusing on *me* by booking girlfriend trips, indulging in shopping therapy, and exercising at least three times a week. I had to remember that I can't be a good mother, a wife, a daughter or a friend; if I am not good to myself first. The most important part of self-care is refusing to condone negativity. Life has undeniable worth and until that is acknowledged, uncaring souls will physically and mental invade your space.

Saving My Sister

Sisterhood is a powerful force for change and healing. We have a duty as women to empower each other, but it's imperative that you save yourself *before* you try to save others. When you're emotionally and mentally out of harm's way, decide how to go back and rescue your sisters. Life-changing knowledge should be in constant rotation between women; we are a gift to each other. We are healers and there is no greater love than that of a woman who is in your corner.

Share the Load

Depression can be cured when you learn to lean into other people. All my positive memories of coming out from the times of darkness have been when other people showed up to carry me and get me through to the other side. I learned throughout depression that I am surrounded by people who love me and want me to be better. Often we assume that it's easier for us to do it all ourselves, but we have to remember the long-term effects of that behavior. We must ask for and accept help, because we need and deserve it.

Seek Professional Help

I treasure my monthly talk therapy sessions—they are my lifeline. It's an opportunity for me to speak my pain, my struggles, my gains and losses. I've learned to let the tears flow and to slow down. Seeking help with a mental health professional to confide in and ask direction from, can mean the difference between life or death.

Through it all, I've learned that I'm a fighter. If I can make it through the darkness, then I can get through anything. This is, by far, the most beautiful part of my diagnosis. Some days are still hard. Some mornings are still slow and threatening. The threats are empty though because I know the way home now. I had to find my voice amid intense personal grief. I had to sit with myself and ask some hard questions. I had to come back to what it was that made my life meaningful.

I hope these words will change your life as they did mine.

ABOUT

Elizabeth Bautista

Elizabeth Bautista is the Manager for the Operations Technology Group at the US Department of Energy Office of Science's NERSC computational facility at the Lawrence Berkeley National Laboratory. She and her team ensure 24/7 accessibility, reliability, and security of the non-classified High Performance Systems, data storage systems, and the wide area network called ESnet that supports scientific research and global partner collaborations.

She avidly supports programs that seek to involve women in STEM, (Science, Technology, Engineer, and Mathematics), she champions staff retention policies, diversity and workforce development, and advocates that the next generation of STEM professionals be trained through hands-on opportunities and practice.

She helps organize technical conferences for women and diversity, and manages the student internship program at NERSC. In 2015, she was chosen as one of 100 Most Influential Filipina Women in the World™. She has a B.S. in Computer Information Systems and an M.B.A. in Technical Management from Golden Gate University, San Francisco.

In her copious free time Elizabeth can be found at a Disneyland somewhere in the world, running workshops that show elementary school children how to program robots, taking in theater or opera, and traveling to far-flung places, or staying close to home.

Elizabeth can be reached at:

Email:	ejbautista626@gmail.com
LinkedIn:	elizabethbautista
Facebook:	www.facebook.com/ejbautista
Twitter:	@filipinasIC

WHEN THE WITCH TAKES YOUR LIVER

By Elizabeth Bautista

I was in kindergarten when the soldiers arrived. Toting guns they would march up and down our street every night about an hour before sunset. They were loud and civilians were ordered indoors. Anyone caught outside was taken away and questioned. It was fascinating to watch them from a bedroom window but all too soon I'd get pulled away, taken to the hiding place and be told to keep quiet. I wasn't to come out until they said it was safe, and by then it was morning.

During the day, the adults told me I couldn't ride my bicycle outside. They yelled at me to "Get inside!" From our yard, I heard soldiers stop people and ask where they were going or where they were coming from and then offer to escort them "home." I don't remember ever seeing those people again. Young adults in the neighborhood also seemed to disappear. Soon, the only people on the streets were the soldiers.

One night, I woke to the sound of a woman screaming. It seemed to come from a house close to ours. Inside my hiding place I turned on the light and called to my mom and uncle. Mom came, immediately switched off the light, and hushed me to be quiet. I told her I heard a scream, and she said it was the witch flying around at night looking for victims. "It didn't sound like a witch," I said. She explained that witches looked for little girls who didn't use a blanket at night. The witch could see your liver if it wasn't covered and would take it. The screams were from people whose liver she took. A few nights later, I heard more screaming. This time, I pulled a blanket over me so the witch wouldn't see my liver, and hid under my pillow to block the screams.

The following morning, I saw Pinky, one of our neighbors sitting on her front porch. Pinky went to the local college. I walked over to her—she was always nice to me. When she looked up, I saw cuts on her lip. Her face was bruised and one eye was almost shut. There were bruises on her arms and legs. I asked what happened. Before she could answer, my uncle came for me and took me back to our house. I asked him what happened to Pinky. He said, "The witch took her liver. That's what people look like when the witch takes their liver." I was horrified, and knew I needed to make sure the witch didn't get *my* liver.

After the soldiers overran our neighborhood I wasn't allowed to sleep in my room. Before sunset, the adults would take me to the hiding place, a little room behind the wall under the stairway, and tell me not to come out. I was supposed to sleep there until morning. Sometimes soldiers would come into the house after dark. I could see them through a little opening in the wall when the lights were on in the living room. The soldiers would demand food and drink and expect my family to serve them. I didn't know why they kept coming, because mostly they didn't seem to like the food. With food now being scarce, they didn't understand that there weren't a lot of choices. The soldiers would yell and scream and make a mess. My mom would try to calm them down. Usually it worked, but sometimes it didn't. When she couldn't calm the soldiers, they would hit my uncle until he started to look like the girl whose liver was missing.

When it was time for me to go to first grade, the adults decided I should stay at the dorm where it was safer. How I loved school! There were no witches, or soldiers and it was fun to wear a uniform. The grounds were huge and there was lots of space to explore.

School was fun and felt so safe. I didn't look forward to going home on the weekends, not with the soldiers there, or the nightly screaming because of the witch taking livers. Home was a scary place. Soldiers were no longer marching the streets neatly. When I was home, I would see them inside the houses, sitting on the porches smoking, or walking around pointing their rifles, harassing people on the street, or just being mean because someone looked at them too long. Some weekends my mom wouldn't come get me from school. She would send a message to the principal that I need to be kept there for the weekend. I liked having the school grounds to myself. There were some kids there on weekends, but most went home.

One Friday afternoon my uncle came to the school and said we would go into town and get a snack before going home. I thought that was a nice treat. He bought me a popsicle and we sat on a park bench while I told him about the new book I was reading. Eventually we started walking home. As we turned the last corner, I saw a crowd of soldiers on the street. With soldiers blocking the way my uncle walked us down another street so we could get to our back door. Inside our house were more soldiers. My uncle pushed me behind him and started talking to the soldiers. He gave me a basket of fruit, spoke to me in Tagalog and pushed me out the door.

He had instructed me to go "home" next door. That made no sense. Why was he telling me to go home to the neighbor? And why wasn't he speaking to me in English as he usually did? I didn't understand so I asked him in English, what was going on. The soldiers all stopped talking and started asking me questions. They wanted to know who I was. My uncle and Mom were answering for me, saying that I was the neighbor and just needed some fruit to take home. The soldiers said I wasn't allowed to take the fruit, especially since my mom didn't know how to cook.

The soldiers ordered my uncle to bring me to them. There were about five soldiers and they all smelled of alcohol. There was partially eaten food on the table and lots of beer bottles. One soldier started talking in Tagalog and touching my hair. It made my skin crawl. I told him he smelled and to stop touching my hair. My mom immediately apologized for my behavior and the soldier just laughed, saying something about teaching me to respect my elders. He took my arm and started dragging me toward the living room where there were more soldiers sitting around. As we entered the room, they all sat up and the soldier said I was tonight's entertainment.

The soldiers started to crowd around. I was scared. My uncle came over and told them that I knew how to dance, except I didn't. The only "dance" I knew was from the program I had been rehearsing for the Christmas musical. He put on the record of the "Little Drummer Boy," and I did my part of the routine. At the end of the song, they all clapped. I bowed, my uncle spoke to them, then quickly took me away. My mom walked me outside and to the neighbor's house. She told them what happened and all the adults agreed that I was very lucky, which I didn't really understand. She asked the neighbor to hide me until morning and either she or my uncle will pick me up to take me back to school. That night there was more screaming: the witch must've been attacking many women. I put my fingers inside my ears to drown out the sounds. I began to doubt the screaming had anything to do with witches, but didn't understand what was happening. I was glad when they took me back to school the next morning.

At the end of the school year, I didn't want to go home. Every night during summer vacation, I was told to hide in the room behind the stairs. Sometimes I thought I heard firecrackers. Later I learned it was soldiers or rebels firing gunshots in our town. Sometimes, someone wounded would be brought into the house and the adults would bandage him up. They were gone by morning, regardless of whether they survived or not.

I was relieved to go back to school for second grade.

One night, while doing my homework by flashlight in the small room, I realized I had left a book in the living room. I peeked through the opening and saw the soldiers, as usual. I kept checking until finally there were gunshots outside and they all left. I moved quickly through the small passageway, down the stairs and grabbed the book. I was almost back to the stairs when I felt someone grab and lift me over his shoulder. He smelled bad and he was saying to some soldiers that he caught me. The other soldiers came back in laughing and said something about entertainment. I said I only know how to dance one song. He stood me up and told me to dance. There was no music so I hummed the music and went through the steps of the "Little Drummer Boy."

When I was finished, I grabbed my book, said thank you and started to excuse myself. The soldiers said I needed to embrace them. I refused. One soldier grabbed my arm, pulled me toward him and put his hands up my dress. I screamed and tried to get away from him. But the more I squirmed the more he tightened his grip. The others were cheering him on. I didn't know what was happening but he was trying to take off my top, and I kicked and screamed. Now I realized that the screaming I had heard during the long nights wasn't from the witches taking a girl's liver. It was from the soldiers trying to hurt them. I wasn't going to allow it. I kept kicking and screaming. He was now trying to get another soldier to hold my arms down so he could take off my underwear. I screamed until my throat hurt, but the laughter and the noise from the soldiers drowned my screams. Suddenly I felt pain on my face, and I began to lose consciousness. Then I heard a gunshot and it seemed like the sky was falling on me.

When I woke up, my head and body hurt and there was something sticky on my shirt. Did the witch take my liver after all? Did the soldiers take my liver? My uncle was leaning over me. He said I fought the soldiers bravely, and had caused enough distraction that nothing happened to me. Nothing happened? Then why did I feel so much pain? Why couldn't I speak? My uncle said he was taking me to a safe place, and to be brave because we would travel at night to avoid the soldiers. My mother, uncle, and I walked a long time. When they saw soldiers, they told me to hide in an empty building. Then they would get me and we'd resume walking. At one point, while waiting for a bus, I moved the scarf off my face to see my reflection and see why it ached so much. I looked like Pinky. *This is what it looks like when they take your liver*, I thought.

The safe place was at my aunt's house. She called a doctor, who after arriving asked a lot of questions, touched different parts of my face, arms, and legs. He said nothing was broken. Then he asked if the soldier put himself inside. I didn't understand what that meant and I couldn't remember. He asked my aunt to examine me while he left the room. She asked me to tell the truth. I said I couldn't remember.

My aunt told my mother and uncle it didn't look like I'd been raped and I was lucky. But by the time my uncle had reached me the soldiers had removed my blouse and pulled my skirt up. One of them punched me in the face—which is why I had a black eye and didn't remember anything. Pinky heard my screams, came from her house, grabbed one of the soldier's guns and shot the soldier who was raping me. It was the soldier's blood on my chest. My uncle and mother knew it was time to leave.

A few months later we were on our way to America. Looking back, I realize how fortunate I was to escape the horrors that no person should ever experience. My eight-year-old self had found refuge in books and learning. It was my happy place. I was an early reader and somehow there were always wonderful books to devour. I loved adventure stories because they took me to faraway places and I imagined myself as the heroes: an astronaut landing on the moon, a traveler stumbling on a magical cave, or a heroine battling a cyclops.

Boarding school was another safe and happy place—safe from assaults, the noise of war, and people who wanted me to do things I knew were wrong. The school grounds were quiet and calming. I could walk safely and occasionally staff kept me company.

Today, when faced with the most challenging issues, I know how to remove myself and go to a happy place. Happy places are the opera or the theater. I still bury myself in adventure stories, and the classics whisk me away to piquant dream states. I love history and traveling to the places described so colorfully in many of the books I read; to experience the castles and alleys that capture my imagination. Or, I spend a day or two at a Disney park to soar on the thrilling rides, dress up as a princess, and visit with my favorite characters.

These activities clear my head and rebalance me for whatever happens in real life. As that eight year old, did I visualize happy scenes and escapes as self-preservation against the screams of neighbors being sexually assaulted and to muffle the gunshots on our street? Today I also wonder whether I imagined myself flying on a magic carpet to a far-off land because that was the only way my eight-year-old self knew how to cope.

Challenges I face today pale in comparison to escaping a developing country under siege, governed by martial law, a place where soldiers used rape to sow fear, control the population, and for entertainment. Whenever I feel something is tough or seems hopeless, I remind myself of what it took for me to get to this point, relieved that the screams of the women being attacked by witches stealing their livers, are gone.

—— ABOUT ——
Charron Monaye

Award-winning playwright/author/coach /entrepreneur and writer, Charron Monaye is living the life she prayed for. Using her extraordinary gifts, Charron has developed a following among aspiring entrepreneurs and writers who seek her knowledge and life lessons on an array of subjects.

Her body of work spans over two decades to include: 5 published books, 3 co-author books, and 2 written and produced theatrical productions. She is currently a lifestyle blogger for MadisonJaye.com. In addition, her writings can be found in 11 book and poetry anthologies across the world and she has been hired to adapt 3 books and 1 life-story into theatrical productions. Understanding the importance of reaching back and helping others achieve their goals, she has made it her mission to help other entrepreneurs build their businesses and brands through her company, Pen Legacy, LLC.

Charron has a BA in Political Science from West Chester University, Master's in Public Administration from Keller Graduate School of Management, a Certificate in Paralegal Studies and Life Coaching, and a Doctorate of Philosophy (Humane Letters) from CICA International University & Seminary. Charron is an active member of Zeta Phi Beta Sorority, Inc. and Order of Eastern Star.

Website:	www.penlegacy.com
Email:	info@penlegacy.com
Facebook:	penlegacyco
Instagram:	iamcharronmonaye
Twitter:	PenLegacy
LinkedIn:	Charron Monaye, MPA

PRAISE GOD! I DON'T LOOK LIKE WHAT I'VE BEEN THROUGH

By Charron Monaye

When I look in the mirror today, I see a woman who prayed, sacrificed, and diligently worked overtime to become an Amazon bestselling author, an award-winning author, an award-winning playwright, a part of the Literary Takeover Authors that signed in New Orleans, LA during Essence Festival in 2017; who received a Doctorate of Philosophy (Humane Letters) from CICA International University & Seminary, and who is the founder of a successful and profitable literary company, Pen Legacy, LLC. When I look in the mirror, I see a woman who gave up living to enjoy life like the average, everyday person and became committed to living a life of her dreams, while doing what she loved to do. That woman in the mirror is the fruits and rewards of being too ambitious to settle and too determined to be comfortable. But the journey to who I see now was far from pretty, colorful, and easy. The difference between who I used to be and who I am today is that I now understand the power in Delay! And the appreciation of being Denied! What God has for me, is for me! I had to constantly remind myself that he doesn't need my help, only my faith and the ability to listen.

On November 29, 2008, I stood in front of a judge accepting a charge that did not belong to me. I did this to honor a man that vowed to be an honest and loyal provider but failed to pay our rent for three months. Now you may ask, "Why didn't you pay it, Charron?" My answer is I was unemployed and unaware. After I had our baby boy, my ex-husband begged me to quit my job and stay at home to take care of our son. He promised to handle all the bills and to provide for the boys and me, and I believed him. But not even a year after that promise, I stood alone in a courtroom pleading for the judge to give me thirty more days to pay the past due amount of $2,978.52 that my husband told me he had paid but hadn't. After hearing the judge's decision, I owned my verdict and let out an "ugly" cry because not only did I receive a judgment against me, I didn't have the $2,978.52 that I promised to pay. But because I knew a God that said, *Let not your heart be troubled: ye believe in God, believe also in me*, I was at peace.

I have a gift and a purpose that I did not fully tap into and in that moment I thought, *you are more than a conqueror, this challenge can only bless you forward.*" It was in that storm that I realized it was time for me to pick up my pen and paper and use my gift to inspire, motivate, and prevent others from going through what I just endured. All of my dreams of publishing my first book were delayed because not only did I have to get $2,978.52 to prevent us from being homeless, I was now a divorced single mother with two sons who looked up to me to protect them. I did not have the money to follow a dream or the credit to see it through, so I wrote my story in my composition book and submitted my manuscripts until a traditional publisher or a small press book company believed in me.

My big break came in 2010 when Yulonda Brown of Purposeful Publishing called and agreed to publish my work. But, as I soon learned, everything comes with a price; a price that I could not afford. But I sacrificed every dime I had to pay for the opportunity. My desire and thirst to want to be everything people said I would never be, made me deplete not only my bank account but my idea of average living. In my mind, I was destined to be a great writer whose name would appear in lights. I would go to bookstores and imagine that my books where on the shelves next to Iyanla Vanzant's books. I made it clear what and where I wanted to be, but the journey I took to get there to make it my reality was full of unhealthy decisions, wasteful spending, grinding instead of strategic planning, and accepting every opportunity that kept me busy, but not aligning me toward my dream in a cost effective manner. I paid for "exposure" that promised new clients, books sales, and partnerships, but the only exposure it provided was my desperation of being seen to prove a point to those who doubted me, or challenged my ability to make this dream come true.

When my first book, *My Side of the Story* was released, you'd think that I'd embrace the moment of being a published author, instead I started a new project of adapting my book into a play and getting it produced. I jumped from project to project, spending, delaying, and setting myself back with debt, avoiding collection calls, and watching my children eat while I drank water because I had sacrificed my dinner for what I thought would make me successful: validation from others that I was doing a great job. Every opportunity I jumped into, I fell back thirty steps. And as a result, I made myself a prisoner to misery, brokenness, and disappointment. These setbacks clouded my ability to see clearly and I began to move on impulse without a successful plan. Now don't get me wrong, accomplishing everything I have to this point made me successful, but it didn't provide enough substance to make me credible. I was writing books, plays, song lyrics, blogs, and articles for CNN iReport, but I wasn't making a mark or leaving quality work that generated revenue or clients. In 2013, after having released two books and writing and producing two stage plays, God bankrupted my vision. He emptied my willingness to do anything else that was, in retrospect, denying me the ability to be who I am as "a writer." Even though I was writing and getting exposure, I wasn't being authentic and honest with my readers, and most importantly, with myself. I was also in a relationship with a man who needed and demanded my attention to focus on his rap and writing career.

Between handling his affairs, being a mother, an employee (yes, I was working full time), and everything to everybody, I was nothing to myself, thus, I had nothing really to offer. I had a voice but using it to fulfill what others needed from me was always way more important than using it to fulfill my needs. I was caught between my lack of finances and not being true to myself, so God stopped the journey and I went back to being average. Now we know, I'm too ambitious to be average, but I was too broke and in debt to be blessed. God said NO! Plus every credit card was maxed out, I had no savings, my credit score was in the 500's, I was living paycheck to paycheck, and had a business that was broke. I was truly the definition of "broke, busted, and disgusted," but with an award-winning play and other honors. I just knew that my journey was over so I pretended to enjoy the average life of going to work and coming home, doing overtime, and paying bills. Now, I needed to pay bills but, when every penny you get has to go to bills and not a Pepsi, it's time to regroup.

I settled into this denial and slowly gave up on Pen Legacy, the company I had created, and on my writing because it was not like people were rushing to the stores to buy my books, anyway. June of 2014, I was forced to move out of the house I was renting from my brother who I thought owned it, but was actually subletting it to me. We'd literally moved into the house six months prior and I was living paycheck to paycheck trying to build Rome in a day and also to pay the rent and the bills, and I was told to leave. I had no money and bad credit. This moment reminded me of that day back in 2008 when I was in housing court fighting not to be evicted and all I kept thinking was, *how in the world did I get back here?* But this time, I prayed hard asking God for direction. I was tired of chasing a dream and a relationship that only led me back to where I promised myself I would never be again. When I finished having a conversation with God, my mother called me and said, "Your aunt is moving into a nursing home and they're willing to let you move into her house but your boyfriend can't move in with you!" My God! Just like that, I had a home in a suburban area that I'd always wanted for my boys and the fact that my boyfriend couldn't move in with me pretty much ended our relationship. It was in this moment, that I took a step back and let God lead the way. I found that I was no longer anxious. Instead, I took time in my new home to find peace and to find myself.

In my rediscovery, I learned just how lost I was in my life. I was living and accepting so much—just to be loved and liked—that I forgot that the only person who I should be living for is ME! In order for me to get to the truth of who I was, I had to uncover and accept who I was *not* and why I needed this kind of validation from others. This period of my denial was the most humbling time of my life because I forced myself to take ownership of my actions. I could no longer blame my boyfriend, my brother, my ex-husband, my dad, or anyone else. I had to blame myself because I allowed their words or actions to, indirectly or directly, affect my choices and my life. I had to constantly remind myself that I am the owner of my life and people have only done to you, what you've allowed. After that realization I began to learn WHY and HOW I was going to change.

A good friend, Vaughn McNeill challenged me and further made me see just how much I was also delaying my progress. Between God's denial and my delay, it was time for me to make some serious changes. After two years of praying, learning, and fixing my life and mindset, everything about my life began to take a new direction. It was like I had gone to sleep in a horrible thunderstorm and woken up in sunshine. In 2015, I wrote my third book, *Love the Real You* and published it under my own publishing company. It made me an Amazon Bestselling Author for two weeks. This book and period in my life, proved that if we want to compete in a marathon, we must train, learn, and prepare for the race *before* actually running. This was the biggest mistake and reason why I had delays and denials, I failed to train, learn, and prepare for the life I desired. I knew what I wanted, but I ran with my heart and not with my head. I hadn't fully planned for success, which led to failure. By writing *Love the Real You* and seeing clearly for the first time, my problems, lacks, and desires, I was able to use what I'd learned to start rebuilding my happily ever after. Which turned out to be a happily ever after that finally made sense! I had peace, good credit, and a company that was flourishing. People started believing in my writing again and I began publishing books, adapting books into scripts, and coaching others to their own successful ending. People believed in me, because for once, I believed in me!

I no longer made hasty decisions because of desperation. I hired three business coaches who provided me with strategic insight when making business decisions and creating profitable programs and projects. I was working smarter, not harder! But wait there's more! Just when I thought the blessings were done, God brought me a man who not only encourages me to be me, no matter how silly or moody, he motivates and loves me. He celebrates my business and instead of me focusing on him, he takes the time to cater and focus on me. I can talk about my day, discuss business deals, or watch *Homeland* and eat his famous salmon and kale greens and be still.

This is what happens when you stop running around and let God direct your path. Stopping my journey was the best thing he could've done for me, because at the rate I was going I could not have received the blessings that I have now because I wouldn't have appreciated them. My children are the happiest they've been in a long time and I'm on cloud nine. For these blessings I must say that I appreciate my journey from the valleys to the mountaintops because I now know the consequences of my actions and where a wrong turn can take me. When I was forced to move from the house my brother was subletting to us, I said to myself, "Charron, you haven't learned the lesson of your ways, because you're repeating your mistakes. You've been here before."

Today, I'm not repeating any mistakes I'm progressing. I honesty have everything I've ever prayed for, plus more. Although my journey was full of failures and losses, my true success only arrived after I turned my delay into a mindset transformation. I used that downtime to fix my life and so can you. Setbacks and failure, doesn't mean it's over. It is, however, a reminder that God needs your attention so he can position you in a way that will grant your every desire.

I pray that after reading this, you are inspired to train, learn, and prepare yourself for your race of life. Your delay is *not* your denial; it is actually the start of your legacy!

Written for Your Breakthrough.

Charron.

ABOUT

Nikeisha Johnson

I am a Captain in the United States Army, a wife of CW3 Anthony Johnson, a mother, a college professor, a minister, a motivational speaker and a current doctoral student. I have served in many different countries and enjoy advocating for others who have not yet identified their own strength. I currently hold a A.A. in Social Psychology B.S in Psychology, M.A. in General Psychology, M.S. in Clinical Psychology and in my last year of Doctorate School. My passion is to encourage, empower, and restore all who have been broken, wounded and torn. My greatest desire is to help others understand the uniqueness of the gift that God has placed within them even before they were shaped in their mother's womb. God has assigned me a mission to help all *"Embrace Your Uniqueness."* For God affording you the opportunity to live is not by mistake but it is his divine purpose for you to prosper even as your soul prospers!

For more information or for future engagements:

Emails: embraceyouruniqueness@yahoo.com
             nsj1@yahoo.com

Facebook: Nikeisha Johnson

PURPOSED JOURNEY FOR A PROMISED DESTINY

By Nikeisha S. Johnson

JOURNEY BEGINS

I was born to two of the most amazing people in the world, yet two of the most functionally challenged people in the world. Alcohol consumed my parents and Metro County Jail was my mother's second home. Because of that many people counted us OUT and had very minimal expectations for not only my parents, but also for me and my brother. That in itself was a weight that had automatically become my burden. It was a burden I sought diligently to lighten for my family. I began to embrace my parents inability, as my ability to dig deep as I clung to their words that gave them hope that "greater" was ahead of me because "greater" was ahead of them. They may not have had multiple college degrees or been as articulate as others, but they possessed something within that would take them further than any that surrounded them. God graced them both with a gift that my father refers to as "THAT IT." It is the gift of servitude that makes God smile, along with the ability to influence, empower, and impact every one they encountered. This too became my gift!

Many people sought to identify all the bad in our life and tried to emphasize all that we lacked outwardly, while they missed what we possessed internally. So much so, that some of those same people had predetermined what the future held for me, which looked nothing like the promises God had shown me. With hidden courage and an undiscovered strength, I countered that expectation by deciding I would be the one in my family to change the game, not only for myself but also for us all. I decided that "greater" was meant for me, but the adversarial pressures weighed on me as I searched within myself and asked, "How could I be greater? God knew the answer to my question even before I asked it. Remember: God says ask and ye shall have and as his children (as the King's kids) he would never tell us to ask if he didn't have the answers.

Soon, I discovered that our lives would change forever. God allowed something that brought change and dependency upon him forever. All from an unexpected knock on the front door. This was no ordinary knock. This was a knock that intentionally brought change! This was a knock that saved not only my mother from herself, but also every trap set by the adversary for our entire family. This knock once answered was the knock that took our mother away. This knock was an arrest for my mother, to take her to a place where she would spend some unplanned time away from my father, my brother, and me, which was more time away than she ever had to spend before. As the police made the arrest my mother looked at us and said, "All is well and it will be all right." While I could not understand it then as a child, I better understand it now as an adult. What was happening was what she needed to get her to her destiny, in order for me to reach mine.

However, this did not look like the promise God had shown me! Weeks went by before my mother returned but when she did we could tell that something had changed for the good. She made herself a promise that she was never going back to that place again. Soon after my mother and father gave their lives to Christ and that's when I saw a better path that would lead me to where I needed to go. My parents taught me different principles that included the ultimate keys to reach my destination. These keys could unlock any door in my life no matter how difficult, but most importantly, it was a set of keys that unlocked God's promises. The main key is PRAYER (the super key that fits all locks) it unlocks the key of FAITH (master key) and the key of faith unlocked the door to my DESTINY that included me joining the Army. That's when my life as an adult set in and my journey was altered.

ALTERED JOURNEY

Being the oldest child and adulthood quickly approaching, I decided to join the military to better assist my family and be able to go to college. This was the biggest decision I'd ever had to make at that point and it stretched me beyond my imagination. Keeping the promises of God in mind, I couldn't help but feel disappointment because it did not look like what God had shown me previously. While I was grateful for the opportunity, depression set in quickly and clouded my life. At that point, years into my career I thought for sure that God had forgotten me. God allowed me to encounter some of the most challenging situations (some I had caused) and some of the worst people, all while hiding me yet keeping me in plain sight. One day after encountering racism, sexism, sexual harassment, rejection from the church, rejection from family and so much more, I decided to call it quits. At that moment I spoke to God because it seemed as though nothing I had dreamt of was coming to pass. Traveling from country to country and from state to state with no family and no one to lean on, made me feel that I had been denied, for whatever reason. I thought feeling unloved, unwanted, unappreciated, misused, and abused was his plan for me. I prayed and asked God to take me home with him. Later that night I went to sleep with the expectation of not waking up the next morning, and when I did wake, I was upset. Since God didn't take me home, I decided to ask my commanding officer during 9/11, to transfer me to a deploying unit so I could go to war because I knew I would not make it back. God stood in the gap then too because my commanding officer told me "NO!" I hadn't realized that he was a Christian until he said, "Specialist, if God wanted you to go he would've made way for you to go, so that he can bring you back. Since he didn't send you neither am I!" Then he said, "Typically when soldiers volunteer those are the ones that don't normally return."

I turned around and slowly walked away, angry as ever but not revealing my true intent. Later that night, I spoke with God again, except this time I came with a heart of repentance. I said, "God I am sorry that I'm not who you showed me you wanted me to be, please forgive me and take me with you," HE spoke back and called me by my name and said "I, your Father have had you the whole time, EVEN IN YOUR LACK I AM FAITHFUL!" At that moment something changed within me in a way I'd never experienced before. That night, I rested in peace knowing that even when I felt as though I was breaking, God still kept me. He was the Potter and I was the Clay! I allowed God to center me and from that day forward, I chose to trust God even when I can't trace him because I know that He is with me and God being *for* me is more than the whole world being against me.

THE NOW PROMISE

I could finally see the promise just as God had previously shown me. He showed me dreams and visions just as he had done before, except this time the dreams and visions began to manifest before my very eyes. The manifestation of the promises aggravated many because they could not and cannot understand how God brought me over. His promise to me is that I will prosper just as my soul prospers; and that you will prosper even as your soul prospers. I saw his blessings first in my career. The more soothsayers spoke against me the more God elevated me. When someone told me, I can't, God said, "Yes you can because I AM going to give it to you!" With that reassurance from my Creator, I stand today in the Army with a Holy boldness, as a Commission Officer, as one of the very few Black American female soldiers. God also allowed me to see myself as a doctor, as a wife, as a mother, and as an author speaking to nations. Although the journey has not been easy, I must testify that each promise has been fulfilled or is being fulfilled. So my friends, be of good courage and reassured in knowing that our Father who art in heaven has not forgotten you nor the promises he has made you, for the master knows the plans that he has for you. The Lord has thoughts of peace and not of evil, to give you an expected end for your purposed journey and to get you to your promise destination. Amen.

ABOUT

Kimberly Jenkins-Snodgrass

Creative, innovative, tenacious and fearless, Kimberly Jenkins-Snodgrass has worked in many areas of national and international entertainment development and production. Her twenty-year career and expertise in Business Artists Management, Special Event Coordination, Public Communications, and Social Activism, is an ongoing representation of her ability to successfully meld Entertainment and Social Activism to create awareness and engaging dialogues through productions that offer thoughtful, historical perspectives, and context. Her passion for the entertainment industry began while serving as an NCO in the United States Army. It was after her military service that veteran Jenkins-Snodgrass partnered with Kitson & Associates in 2009 to secure talent and sponsorship for the historic Sojourner Truth Unveiling held at the U.S. Capitol—Emancipation Hall. The capacity event participants included First Lady Michelle Obama, former Secretary of State Hillary Clinton and former Speaker of the House Nancy Pelosi. Kimberly (aka Stargazer) was also a columnist for *Jack the Rapper*, the first Black music trade magazine.

Ms. Jenkins-Snodgrass is a tireless advocate for justice, civil and human rights. During her partnership with the late Justice Warrior, Joyce Ann Brown, and her family's personal struggle to see justice served, she has traveled the country fighting wrongful incarceration. She has also educated communities about Mothers (Fathers) for the Advancement of Social Systems Inc. (MASS). It is a successful and proven reintegration to society program. When Ms. Jenkins-Snodgrass experienced the injustice firsthand with her son's wrongful incarceration, her faith in the system was lost. However, her story is one that far too many American families experience and it has strengthened her resolve to work for equality. She is a partnering consultant at MASS and board member of Interfaith Action Human Rights (IAHR).

Twitter:	@kimjsnodgrass
Facebook:	Kimberly Jenkins-Snodgrass
Instagram:	kimberlyjenkinssnodgrass
Email:	dbnd2.kimberly@gmail.com

Kimberly would like you to help Interfaith Action for Human Rights (IAHR) end the abuse of solitary confinement in Virginia and Maryland. Please visit www.interfaithactionhr.org.

OVERCOMING TAG TOE FEAR

By Kimberly Jenkins-Snodgrass

On January 9, 2003, my son Kevin D. Snodgrass Jr. affectionately known as KK, was socializing with his childhood friend when tragedy struck. They were both only twenty-two years old. It happened at KK's rented townhouse, in Woodbridge, Virginia. Someone fired a flurry of gunshots through the townhouse windows. KK's friend, Maurice McKoy, twenty-two, was shot in the head and killed while playing PlayStation. The cold-blooded murder rocked the quiet suburban community and devastated both the McKoy family and KK.

It took Prince William County police, investigators, and prosecutors approximately one year to bring the suspected killers to trial. O'Bryan D. Woods, twenty, a student at Virginia Tech and Antonio J. Shaw, twenty-three, were indicted on charges of first-degree murder; Romayan K. Robinson, twenty-two pleaded guilty to voluntary manslaughter and weapons charges. All were African Americans who were publicly charged and brought to trial. Deals were made in exchange for testimony and Woods who drove the car— walked free after giving testimony against Antonio Shaw. But, it wasn't over. There was another person allegedly involved. A thirty-year-old Caucasian man named Jeffrey "White Boy Jeff" Rasmussen was later arrested and charged with possession of a firearm by a twice convicted felon, shooting into an occupied vehicle, murder, shooting into an occupied dwelling, use and display of a firearm. He was released on $1,000 bail, attended Shaw's trial but never testified, the murder charge was abandoned, *nolle processed*, and he was later released on work-release for the remaining charges.

Prosecutors publicly stated, and local media reported, that KK was the intended target in retaliation for a neighborhood "fistfight" that had occurred earlier that day.

The foundation for every life changing event is laid long before it occurs.

I had never lived in fear until December 19, 2006 when KK was arrested for the murder of Jeffrey M. Rasmussen. On notification of KK's arrest, I mentally engaged in tag-toe fear. The proper term is toe tag. The slang term used in the prison system is tag toe. Meaning a mother or family member receiving their loved one back with a tag on their toe.

For several months after KK's arrest and leading up to his trial, I suffered from panic attacks when having thoughts that KK could've been delivered to me with an identification tag hanging off one of his toes. Since the late 90's African-American communities nationwide had become victims of systemic police shootings during arrests at an overwhelming rate. Once I learned that KK was arrested on a no-knock warrant and heard how the arrest had physically taken place, with the cops barging in, I knew my son was only alive by the grace of God.

After a sleepless night, early the next morning the doorbell rang and there stood Marilyn, Juanita, Shirley, and Deborah who came conveying prayer and the purest form of sisterly love. We were all members of the National Congress of Black Women (NCBW), Prince William Virginia Chapter. We prayed and talked for hours. This visit was instrumental in me finding my reset button to face family, friends, and professional colleagues. The shame of being in this situation was minimized. The fear had subsided and both my physical and mental strength had been restored from this extraordinary expression of sisterhood.

In 1978, I had graduated from Alliance high school in Ohio and was due to return home to Chicago in a couple of weeks. Sitting in the Cantel Elks lodge in Alliance, Ohio, with close friends Diane and Shelia—the two teased me about being sexually inactive and dared me to engage a guy named Kevin who was standing at the bar across from our table. Alliance is a very small town and both Diane and Shelia had known Kevin since they were kids. Our one-night stand was memorable for both of us and my last days in Ohio were spent going on platonic dates with Kevin. Before my departure, I gave Kevin my Chicago number and left for home as planned. A couple of months went by and one day I came home to a telephone message from Kevin. I returned the call and we started talking long distance and eventually made plans for him to come visit me in Chicago. During the visit he formally met the Jenkins family. I later moved back to Ohio and after living with Kevin for a year, we had a huge falling-out and I decided I wanted more out of life than shacking up and working a low-income sales job at JC Penney, finishing college on my parent's dime was out because I hadn't listened to their terms when I graduated high school at the age of sixteen.

Long story short: I eventually joined the Army, and Kevin followed me and we left Ohio together. I became a soldier, later married the one-night stand, becoming a wife way too early and shortly thereafter a mother. By time I was twenty years old, I had been married two years, and was about to give birth.

While home on military maternity leave visiting my parents, who lived on the Southside of Chicago, I reconnected with childhood friends Lisa and Myrdis. The three of us had been apart for a couple of years but there we all stood in our final trimester enduring the month of June and Chicago's scorching heat while waiting anxiously to see who would give birth first. We all had boys, I came in second place giving birth to Kevin Duane Snodgrass Jr., on July 15, 1981. The Lord blessed me with a healthy beautiful baby boy who was simply perfect in both Kevin and my eyes.

My first separation from my son KK came ninety days after his birth. Good old Uncle Sam called both Kevin and I to serve overseas in Frankfurt, Germany. My husband was deployed first, while I stayed in Chicago caring for Kevin Jr. However, it became inevitable that I had to get on that damn plane! My parents and best friend Diane took over loving and nurturing Kevin Jr., until we were reunited four months later in Frankfurt, Germany. Once our eyes connected and I inhaled his scent, I vowed never to be separated from my son again!

My overseas tour was coming to an end and I had received orders reassigning me to the Pentagon in Washington, D.C. Kevin Sr., had exited the Army while we were in Germany and his orders returned him to his home state of Ohio—Uncle Sam did not give a darn that we were married and had a small child. Of course, we could've paid for Kevin's travel at our own expense, but on a sergeant's salary, the latter was the best option. It was a no-brainer that KK would travel with me because we were never separated more than a normal workday once Diane brought him to me overseas. While in Germany, KK's babysitter Ms.

Audrey took the first initials from Kimberly and Kevin and nicknamed Kevin Jr., KK. This nickname would stick with him into his adulthood.

In 1984, I landed at Washington National Airport with KK in my arms. Waiting at the airport was my dad "Papa Joe" who had driven twelve hours from Chicago to make sure KK and I arrived back in the U.S. safely and had family waiting to greet us after the long flight home. I hadn't seen my father in three and a half years, which was way too long… I was truly a Daddy's girl! During in-processing at Fort Myers, Virginia, I learned that there was a waiting list for on-base housing at both Fort Myers and Fort Belvoir. I was so excited to be back safely on U.S. soil and after living on post in Germany, I wanted nothing to do with military on-base housing. I took the hiccup as a sign from God and without hesitation I just kept things moving with KK in tow. Dad and I searched unfamiliar terrain for living accommodations for my family. During this time Dad and I enjoyed the rich history of "Chocolate City" Washington, D.C. Due to today's gentrification, "Chocolate City" is no longer chocolate! I watched Dad bond and become acquainted with his grandson, we talked and laughed as we revisited our late 60's family trip to Washington, D.C., during the Civil Rights era.

After searching for about a week, we found a nice affordable two-bedroom apartment in Falls Church, Virginia. Once moved in, my husband arrived after reconnecting with his family in Ohio. After a couple of years of living in Falls Church, we purchased our first home in Woodbridge, Virginia. I was twenty-six and Kevin was twenty-nine. I thought the D.C., Maryland and Virginia (DMV) metropolitan area was the perfect location to build a family, raise kids, and pursue my career goals. Employment was plentiful and the public education system was highly ranked in the nation. Northern Virginia terrain reminded me of Frankfurt, Germany. The state landscape was very clean and you rarely heard about any violent crimes being committed in the area. I was sure there could be no better military assignment than the Washington metropolitan area.

In the coming years, I would convince my parents, brothers, and sisters to leave both Chicago and Dallas and move to Virginia so we all could be together. Thirty years later, my eldest sister Joanne who is blind, has never forgiven me for orchestrating the huge family move. I never considered how dramatic and overwhelming such a move would affect Joanne since she had been trained to maneuver Chicago independently and the move caused her to leave longtime friends behind.

I quickly learned that you can't live in the metropolitan area without becoming both socially and economically aware. By this time the crack cocaine epidemic was on both the East and West Coast. It had penetrated African-American communities, destroying families throughout the United States. For two decades crack babies were being born, children were being orphaned, and African-American fathers and mothers were being incarcerated under Presidents Reagan and Bush, and mass incarcerated under President Clinton and the second Bush administration.

December 17, 2006, early that evening, "White Boy Jeff" Rasmussen was murdered while parking his car near his home. Five hours later at approximately 10:30 p.m. two Prince William County detectives knocked on my door. During the interview, I noticed the one cop had coached Pop Warner football with my husband and was KK's former childhood coach. This officer took the lead in questioning as if we all were still friends. We didn't know how serious the visit really was.

Detective: Have you heard from KK?

Me: Not since earlier today. Why?

Giving no response to my "why" inquiry the Detective followed up with...

Detective: Do you know if KK has been in a fight?

Me: No. What is this about?

Detective: Well, if you see KK have him call us.

The other detective, looking stupid as hell was more into the décor and was attempting to walk through my house without a warrant when I directed both of them specifically to the dining room area, while not offering either of them a seat at the table. The detectives quickly picked up on my motherly posturing and recognized that I knew my civil rights and was not afraid of them. Within nanoseconds I shut down their late-night Barney Fife interrogation.

On December 19, 2006, KK was arrested for the murder of Jeffrey M. Rasmussen. My son was charged and convicted of first-degree murder, in two business days by a jury pool that consisted of one sitting black female juror and predominately white male and female jurors. The motive for the murder allegedly was for the revenge of McKoy's murder three years earlier.

This was my first and second red flag concerning the case. At a toned 6'3, 195 pounds, KK was a trained boxer and true fist-fighter type of guy who had no school, juvenile, or adult police record containing weapon charges. The wrongful conviction consisted of prosecutorial misconduct, coerced rehearsed testimony, and ineffective counsel.

The two-day trial included the selection of a jury, the trial, and the jury verdict. After the guilty verdict, my ride-or-die friend Renee was truly crying my silent broken-hearted motherly tears. I couldn't muster a tear in the courtroom. Long ago I learned from being in the military not to waste emotions or time on situations you can't control and at this juncture crying was not going to help my son and family in our legal nightmare.

After receiving the verdict, I remember feeling light as a feather, mentally and spiritually. I was not receiving what the judge was dispensing. I remained calm absorbing all the bullshit that I could not control. Spiritually, I felt the Lord's presence like I had never felt his presence in my adult life before. Once the court was adjourned after the verdict—every courtroom movement was captured in my mind as if it was a slow-motion video. I turned and captured the shock on my husband's face, my younger son Kyle's cry sounded like that of a small child whose hand had been slammed in a door. I saw my eighty-one-year-old mother slowly pushing herself up from her seat while tapping the floor with her cane. She then stepped into the courtroom aisle and blurted out in the soundless courtroom, "you prejudice motherfuckers!" Hearing my mother's words, I smiled and thought, *this is not over... Game on!*

I didn't cry for KK until a year after his conviction, and that was only because I'd finally accepted that proving his wrongful conviction in the Commonwealth of Virginia was going to be both historical and the fight of my life!

KK's case is a non-DNA case, meaning nothing forensically ties him to the crime. A year after his conviction, I had been bamboozled by two incompetent Virginia lawyers, which exhausted both our savings and a portion of our 401k. Since KK's criminal case was not a capital murder case, pro bono legal representation was not knocking on our doors. I finally came to the conclusion that I could burn my own money! I started working and advocating for KK myself on the outside while KK researched case law on the inside.

After all we had gone through, I was not the same person. On one level, I felt mentally strong and my mind had already started to strategize ways to seek KK's freedom. On another level I was exhausted, and hurting from a pain that couldn't be measured or even articulated. Finally, I had a true mother's cry, I cried so hard that I would not cry again until my father's death in April 2010. Moving forward, my focus was solely God, staying healthy, family, and freeing KK. My social life came to a screeching halt and my circle of friends shrank. During this time, I became a firm believer that everything and everyone has a season in your life. I purposely formed a tight circle of friends… when all was done, I would say I had less than five close friends. I didn't need money, I just needed a call or two from those that I had supported and invested in over the years. And, for those who owed me money to pay up in full! At this point, I strongly believed that since I knew God before this storm, and felt his presence during the storm, he would bring both KK and me through the storm.

My efforts to free KK has become a movement within the Jenkins-Snodgrass family, throughout the United States and abroad. The support of true friends and advocates has been tremendous. While I detest what this evil dysfunctional, broken, justice system has done to my family, I see God's work in my life and in KK's life. He's my strongest one. Neither my youngest son Kyle nor my husband could have endured this nightmare. Kyle was sixteen, when this injustice hit our family. The devastation hit him so hard that he was unable to receive his blessing and never answered his acceptance letter from Morehouse College.

For years now, KK and I have worked his criminal case. He's become a very savvy legal mind within the walls. My home office houses his legal affairs. God sent KK an angel by the name of Sister Beth Davies, who visits, advocates, and corresponds with KK regularly while he's in the mountains of Virginia at Red Onion State Prison.

In 2013, we hit another roadblock. KK was placed in solitary confinement and nobody in the Virginia Department of Corrections (VDOC) would give family and interested advocate groups a clear answer why. We were always directed back to the very people who were depriving my son of his basic human rights. Advocating against Virginia solitary confinement is comparable to the Justice Department attempting to penetrate and take down a drug cartel.

It has been written that solitary confinement is "a practice that isolates a person from human contact for 22-24 hours a day. It's a practice that often results in substantial, often irreversible, damage to someone's physical and mental health. There is a growing worldwide consensus that it is ineffective and should be banned."

Since KK's placement in solitary, my "tag toe" fears periodically resurface and I often feel as though I'm fighting a case within a case. The current prison practice of using solitary confinement is one of the United States' worst kept secrets! As a mother, it's a fight I never imagined I would have to wage. However, it's a fight that I am determined to win for KK and others behind the wall who have no voice.

Why does Kevin continue to be in solitary confinement? The reasons are unclear, documentation is inconsistent, and our calls to Virginia state officials go unanswered. This broken justice system is one of the few things that we can't blame on the current Trump Administration. Mass incarceration for African Americans has been the rule for many decades.

The Virginia Department of Corrections (VDOC) cannot and will not police itself. With the support of Interfaith Action for Human Rights (IAHR), we started a Change.org petition that garnered 21,000 supporters nationwide to amplify our voices and let VDOC know that we demand that KK be released from solitary confinement.

We've been told KK could be in solitary confinement until 2020. Of course, I'm not accepting this evil plan. The Western District of Virginia, Fourth Circuit Court of Appeal heard Kevin's pro se filed civil claim August 2017, and we are waiting on the court's ruling.

Those trapped in solitary confinement are voiceless and become invisible. People assume the worst about the convicted who are often no different from you and me and simply made some bad decisions. Some are like my son, innocent and praying the day will come when the truth literally sets them free. I pray that day comes for KK.

Update: "Happy birthday Dad!" KK called home on September 5, 2017, to wish his dad a happy birthday and he shared with him that he was released from solitary confinement earlier that morning on his birthday! While somewhat relieved, Kimberly plans to continue her fight and it is well documented in her soon to be released book, *You Can't Have Him.*

---ABOUT---

Queen Rev. Mutima Imani

Queen Rev. Mutima Imani works to heal the heart of humanity. For over thirty-five years, Mutima has offered healings, spiritual coaching and Rites of Passage programs. She traveled for twelve years with the foremost conference for African American Women on Tour (AAWOT) conducting Coming to Awareness, a rite of passage program for women.

Mutima has a Master's in Public Administration with an emphasis in Phenomenology, the study of the development of human consciousness, self-awareness and how all things work together. She works as Organization Development Specialist providing Executive Coaching, Team Building and Diversity Planning for organizations that understand that their greatest investments are in their employees.

She serves as a Social Justice Minister and activist proclaiming the Divinity in all things and advocating justice for people of the global majority, teaching Restorative Justice practices and principles as a tool for healing harm. She conducts Healing the Wounds of Racism workshops and celebrating diversity dialogues. Mutima is a visiting Professor at JFK University's College of Graduate and Professional Studies and Cross-Cultural in Counseling Psychology at the Pleasant Hill Campus in California. In search of her Native American roots she studied with Pueblo Sanchez a Native American Shaman for six years. Mutima is a Tantra teacher and student studying the Art of Sacred Sexuality. She passionately invokes the Divine Spirit of Love, Kindness and Forgiveness in all of her work.

Email:	thequeenmutima@gmail.com
Phone:	510-205-4069
Websites:	theurbanhealingtemple.com
	www.ParCenTra.com
LinkedIn:	mutima-imani-4810258
YouTube:	Mutima Imani
Twitter:	Mutima Imani@heartfaith
Instagram:	mutimaimani

THE ANCESTORS SAID TO SAY: HEAL

By Queen Rev. Mutima Imani

For many years now I've been being told in my meditations that my ancestors want to speak through me. Both my parents are Ancestors and I feel them with my grandparents on both sides urging me to say and write things that would be of service to my family and the world.

They have told me to tell people that they are Divine expressions of this thing called life, and to stop thinking of ourselves as sinners.

They have said love is available to us all and is a healing salve for all of life's challenges. My Ancestors are so wise and they have had so many important messages for me.

I have heard them say to forgive those who have harmed me, don't let those who harm me take up real estate in my mind. Release them and release the harm for they have already forgotten about that which is eating me up.

So I practice forgiveness. And it is a real gift to my life. For everything I have been denied I have used forgiveness to hold onto my faith. I trust that I am guided, guarded, and protected. I use forgiveness as a healing tool.

I once went to hear a professor from UC Berkeley talk about a book he had written called *Burden of the Chains*. It discussed the abolitionist movement, those few white people who were against the cruelty of slavery. The book told the stories of white women who boycotted sugar to protest against slavery and slave conditions. At the end of the talk a person in the audience asked the professor if he thought African Americans should be given reparation. His answer was NO. When asked why he could say no after spending the last two hours talking about the horrors of the Middle Passage and displaying artifacts of slavery, he said it was his contradiction.

In that moment many people just got up and walked out. I was deeply disturbed and went home to meditation. My Ancestors started telling me to forgive white people for the ways they have distorted history and for the cruelty and hate they have inflicted on the world with their contradictions. I wrote this poem to give voice to my feelings.

It's called *Releasing the Burden of the Chains.*

I forgive you America, my brother who has fallen in sin out of grace
I refused to bear my egg to seed your ugly ways,
to sanction your tactics and methods... your plans for mass
destruction.
I forgive "you" White Power,
for feeding off my breast, sucking my milk,
I helped make you what you are,
And now I say to you no more...
I refused to give birth to the conditions we live in,
all the pain of this Culture of Violence.
And I bring the good news.
I forgive you... now get off my back...
I am releasing the burdens of the chains.
I forgive you, America for all of your racial wounds...
for the horrors of slavery.
I release the terror of the chains.... the fear of the torture....
the agony, the anger, and the pain.
As I look back to witness bodies floating,
eyes being poked out,
my people hanging from trees,
the cries of those being beaten,
backs bleeding,
babies dying,
mothers crying,
dignity being denied.
I forgive you and I take back my power.
I forgive you for all that you have done and are doing.
My intentions and prayers stop you in your tracks,
exposing your contradictions and mine.
I am free, I am free, we are free.
Wake up America, Your power is fading,
I have released the burdens of the chains.
I hold a new vision, one that includes everyone,
freed from the illusions of democracy,
healed from the pain of the past.

In my diversity work, "Healing Racial Wounds," I tell people that it's important to honor the blood that flows through their veins. To explore what is the internalized oppression that comes from our Ancestral wounds and from our life experiences that are impacting their lives.

The most important message from my Ancestors is that my life path supports my life purpose. The ancestors are saying to tell the truth about who I am, the stories of my experiences and upbringing clearly explain who I am today and what is mine to do.

I want to start by sharing a memory I have had, before I was born into this black body. I was in an all-night medicine journey with the late Pablo Sanchez the Native American/Mexican Shaman I worked with for six years. I found myself without a body experiencing complete bliss, riding the bliss wave is how I describe it. I heard from a distance the sound of feet shuffling as a gathering was starting to happen. I stood on the outside of the gathering and leaned in to hear. I heard "there is too much suffering on earth it is time to go and help out." I said, "I am not going!" Then I heard a clearing of a throat. And I said, "I don't want to go 'cause I don't want lose this blissful feeling." Then I heard the voice say, "this feeling is yours and it will also be with you. You just have to remember it." It has taken me many years to find that feeling of bliss. One moment I remember it and then I forget it.

Remembering and forgetting that's the game that I play, I trip so hard I forget who I really am, and then I let love in and love leads the way for me to remember. These are lyrics from a song called "To Remember" by Cornucopia.) I am always reminding myself to stay in my bliss, it is mine and no one can take it away. And I must admit that the pain and suffering I witness can be overwhelming.

My Ancestors invite me to explore why I am feeling or thinking a certain way. Is what I am reacting to happening right now or am I being triggered by past events or experiences that are unresolved in my bloodline or one of my past lives? I once heard, on one of my journeys, "my soul is as old a redwood tree and is filled with ancient wisdom." I believe that the past, present and future are all happening at the same time.

I chose my parents because of the intense love between them. In this life I chose a strong black man as my father. From his lineage I got perseverance, and the ability to put one foot forward no matter what is happening. For my mother I choose a black woman whose spiritual roots taught me not to be afraid. Her mother was a healer and her father was half mixed-race man who passed as a white barber all his life.

I am the proud daughter of Sergeant Clarence E. Lyons and Phyllis June Mauzy. My father was a lifer in the US Air Force. I was my father's first child and my mother's third and for the first eight years of my life I lived overseas. We lived in Casablanca and then in Okinawa I did my first four years of elementary school in Okinawa and then we moved to the Apple Valley in the Mojave Desert in San Bernardino, California. We were the second black family to move into Apple Valley. My father had an adventurous spirit when we lived overseas. We would go on family outings and explore the countryside, or go to the nearest beach. Sometimes we were the first African American and/or Americans that people saw. My mother would always tell me, "Act nice, you are representing America." As a military brat I grew up with a sense of being a proud American.

Most of the time we were given a grand welcome, the red carpet was rolled out for us, we were met with open arms and treated with dignity and pride. But there were a few occasions when we weren't invited in or treated with kindness, when this happened my father never made a fuss, he just got us out of harm's ways. When people weren't being kind my mother would get our attention and say, "Look at me and stop looking around. What is going on is none of your business." My mother and father never told me sister and brothers anything about race or racism. I was seven the first time I heard the word nigger. My youngest brother and I were playing at a playground in Okinawa and a little white boy called me a nigger because he wanted me to give up my turn to swing. I paused because I didn't know what nigger meant and said "Nigger you're a nigger too!" That night at dinner, I asked my father, "What's a nigger?" He got visibility upset and my mother called him out of the kitchen into their bedroom. When they came out again, they didn't say anything and my father didn't answer my question. The next day I pushed the boy around because what he said upset my father, but I still didn't know what the word meant. It wasn't until we moved from Okinawa to the Apple Valley and the KKK started coming on Friday nights and writing the word "Nigger" on the garage door that I realized the word had something to do with the color of my skin.

I believe that my mother and father thought they were protecting us by not talking about race. To this day I have mixed feeling about their approach. I was filled with a deep sense of pride for being an American. I had awareness that I was different, but not inferior because of the color of my skin. I was the first black student for my fourth grade teacher and the only black student in the school besides my younger brother.

Mrs. Kill was her name. She placed me in the back of the room between two unruly boys, these two boys would start to mess around making faces and talking to each other. She'd have her back to the class writing on the broad and when she heard them talking she'd turn around and throw an eraser at me. After the fifth time she hit me in the head in my first week in her class I told my mother who came to school to talk to the principal and my teacher. Mrs. Kill said she was sure it was me because all black students were disruptive and didn't know how to act in class. My mother assured her that I was very obedient. Mrs. Kill didn't know that up to that point I had been a child who did what I was told. Her negative definition of me expanded me outside of the boundaries my parents had set for me. I began to use the power I had as a young black girl living in a white environment. I had teachers who didn't think I could learn, and depending on how I felt, I would either blow their minds by making an effort to be the best student in class, or I'd take a break and ride the wave of low expectations.

I had teachers who knew I was brilliant. They supported and helped me learn to love learning. When I was in the ninth grade I decided that I wanted to be the lead cheerleader. When I told my father it was the first time his response to me was ever doubtful and discouraging. He said you are setting yourself up for disappointment. I was confused but determined to try out and win that position. And I did. There was seven cheerleaders on the team and we would take turns practicing at each other's homes. Every time it was my turn to host practice the same two cheerleaders would always miss practice. It was many years later that I realized that their parents didn't want them coming to my house because I was black. Some of these girls went to elementary school with me and when we got to high school in Social Studies class they would talk about what their parents would say about black people. I remember one girl "my friend" told us that her father said that, as a rule black people would rather buy Cadillacs than soap. When I questioned her, she said, "I'm not talking about you. You're the exception to the rule."

When I was in college, there were incidences when I was too black for the whites and not black enough for the blacks. So I lived pretty much on the outside of the two worlds. My black friends would tease me because of the way that I talked and they would say things like, "What's wrong with you, can't even say the word nigger properly?" It took them a couple of quarters to accept me and once I did get involved with them they would tell me, "Don't take this or that professor, he never gives any person of color anything over a C." What they didn't know was that I had already taken that class and gotten an A. When I thought about that professor I remembered he would call all the students by their last name, adding Mr. or Miss to it. But he never called me by my last name so when I would address him I'd do the same thing. Eventually he started to call me by my last name.

One day he said to me, "You're very ambitious." I thanked him, because no one had ever said that to me. I had learned to treat people the way they treated me. If someone was loving, kind, and friendly to me that's what they got in return. If someone turned their nose up, was mean and rude to me, they would get that from me. There are other stories about difficulties going into restaurants, getting tires changed, or being stopped by the police, where my reactions—because I hadn't been told to expect to be treated poorly because I am black—helped things to turn out favorably. This would always surprise my black friends. Only now, at sixty-two years old that I have admitted how hard it was to grow up the way I did.

My work has mostly been focused on celebrating diversity and healing our racial wounds. I loved teachable moments and I don't find it a burden to explain to white people, why what they said was offensive, and how they can rephrase and restate it so that they can interact in a less racist way. When a white person says to me "I don't see color" (and by the way I've had black people say that to me too) My response is, "I must be invisible to you because I'm standing in front of you proud of the darkness of my skin, loving my blackness." One of my favorite things to do is to stand in front of a crowd of white people and ask them to say, "black is beautiful." I believe because of the way that black has been and is being portrayed that our subconscious mind has—for centuries—associated the word with negativity and evil. Saying black is beautiful is a tipping point healing concept that will erase centuries of negativity toward people who have dark skin and the fear of the feminine womb, which is considered a black hole. Just saying, "black is beautiful" is based on the scientific fact that without the primary color black there would be no other colors.

That simple and profound concept when properly understood could erase centuries of erroneous thinking that would correct and heal the heart of humanity. Healing the heart of humanity is the title of one of my signature lectures, keynote addresses, and workshops. To say "black is beautiful" is the beginning of erasing the collective race conscious wounds of the old lies that purport that Africans are 3/4 of person, unworthy of being treated with dignity and pride. Say "black is beautiful" and claim your divinity.

My dear teacher and friend from Ghana, Brother Ishmael Tettah, has written *The Mission of Jesus Revealed*. This short powerful book proclaims that Jesus was killed, because he had the audacity to say that being human was divine. I am the Son of God and you are the children of God. Claiming our Divinity and living Our Lives from this place of knowing heals the wounds of racism. The affirmation that I often share is, "Black is beautiful and I am a Divine expression of this thing called life." I find that it erases the unconscious and conscious feelings of the shame, the blame, and from the guilt of the crimes of racial injustices. It works for everyone who will dare to use it. I challenge you to listen to your ancestors, claim your divinity, and heal racial wounds. I believe that if we listen to our Ancestors and hear what they have to say, we can be guided to heal them and to build a world for future Generations to experience more harmony on Earth. Healing racial wounds is an inside job that leads to liberation, forgiveness and heals the heart as it opens to accepting the truth. Your Divinity is waiting for you to claim. Claim your Divinity!

I am available to do Individual, Family and Community Healing Circles.

————— ABOUT —————

Margo Southwick

Margo is committed to working, helping, and grooming our youth for today's society. She currently works with TrendATee "Improving Lives One Tee At A Time." This organization is centered on inspiring, educating, and assisting our young people to increase their academic potential and achievement as well as offer authentic learning experiences such as: workshops/academic enhancement/tutorial classes/activities/moral character building and other helpful tools. Margo believes we must keep in mind that interrelated parts are at work here. When our children can think, learn and achieve goals outside the box; they are working toward becoming "Whole Beings." We should keep this quote in mind, "Our children learn with their bodies, their senses, their memories, their perceptional skills and their thinking." — Dr. Patricia Phipps SRA/McGraw Hill. This creates a "win-win" for us all as a nation.

Margo Southwick holds a Bachelor of Arts Degree. She attended the College of Alameda in Alameda California and Texas Southern University in Houston Texas. Margo is a native New Orleanian and currently lives in Texas. She is a mother of two young adult children and an elementary school teacher who enjoys family, friends, writing and storytelling.

Email:	MargoSouthwick@yahoo.com
Phone:	832-798-9077
Twitter:	@Margo_Southwick
Facebook:	Margo Southwick

THE LYING WONDER

By Margo Southwick

It was spring 2003. I was turning thirty-seven years old, married with two children, Lori and P.J. I wouldn't say that I was gullible, but a bit naïve and wanted to believe that what my husband Phillip said was true about anything and everything. He was my safety net, but there was a gaping hole in the net that caused the bottom to fall out! His despicable actions caused disappointment, hurt, betrayal, and all kinds of other emotions during this time in my life. He never considered the impact that his choices would have on our family. But during this time, the one thing I knew for sure was how to pray! I asked God to please don't let me fall. I stumbled and maneuvered through the pain, and God kept me! I didn't have any experience as to how far one would go to cover up a mishap; not a mistake. What happened next would change the trajectory of my life and my marriage.

One day Phillip suggested that I take the children home to visit family for spring break, and he would stay behind because of his work schedule. I was excited about a few things happening in our lives; going home to see my folks; particularly my mom sounded good to me, plus it was my birthday. We had just bought a new car with an awesome finance rate, which meant our credit was building. So yes; I was in a good space and a happy place, or so I thought! Phillip drove us to the airport, we said our "see you later(s)" and the children and I headed to flight check-in. We flew into Houston from Arizona, connected with one of my siblings then drove to New Orleans. We arrived early evening and my folks and I celebrated my birthday with all the food and treats I was unable to enjoy in Arizona. We ate cake from Gambino's, crawfish, authentic Po-boy sandwiches, Sno-balls, Hubig pies and the menu goes on! Phillip called to check-in and I remember my mom picking up and saying, "Margo telephone, it's Phillip, he must be missing y'all!" We had been gone about four days and counting. I chatted with him a bit and nothing seemed to be amiss.

When spring break was over my children and I flew back to Arizona. Once we touched down, I called Phillip to pick us up from the airport; but there was no answer. I called several times, still no answer. He finally pulled up to the flight arrival area in his "scraper;" a box Chevy, a cool car but his needed cosmetic and interior work. I thought, *why is he picking us up in this car and not our new car?* And I made a mental note to ask him about it. We loaded up the car and headed home. On the ride, I looked over at him, he was unshaven and looked sleep deprived. "You look tired what's wrong?" I asked him. He shook his head to imply nothing. "Why did you pick us up in this car?" His response: "We'll talk about it when we get home." *Something must've happened to the car*, I thought. Meanwhile, Lori was in the back seat sighing loudly. She was clearly annoyed because the deal was, when she passed to eleventh grade she would get the Chevy, but this didn't happen.

We arrived home and Phillip and I took this issue to the patio for discussion. Our new car was not at home! He then proceeded to tell me that the car had been stolen. He said that he'd stopped at a store, left the motor running and someone hopped in car and took off! (Lie#1) Phillip looked so sad and seemed too have felt really bad about what had happened. I called the insurance company and filed a claim. My next call was to my mom (in tears), telling her what had happened. Her response to me was, "well Margo don't worry about it you have insurance and can get another car." What I didn't find out until years later was that my mom was trying to comfort me and not make a bad situation worse. Actually, she and my sister (Lydia Ann) were having their own conversation that went something like this:

"Lydia Ann did Margo call and tell you about her car?"

"No I haven't spoken with Margo. Why what happened?"

"Well, she said when she got home Phillip told her he went to a store and left the car running while he ran in and when he came out, the car was gone."

"WHAT?!! Mama you know that doesn't sound right. Who do you know leaves their car running while they run in a store in Oakridge? That sounds like some movie mess."

"I was thinking the same thing." My mom agreed. It was years later that my sister revealed what she and my mom had thought about this madness.

I called the police department every day asking if there were any updates on my car. The dispatcher finally said, "Mrs. Southwick, I'll give you the number to call Officer Sergeant who is, handling your case, for updates, questions or concerns. I promise you, when we find your car we'll contact you." I made a few calls to the officer, left messages and waited for a call-back. Days and nights passed and we fell back into our work and school routine.

One night in particular, I felt a deep sadness swelling within me and I went to bed earlier than usual. I woke when Lori came into the room with the phone and said, "Mom a man named Robert is asking to speak to you." I'll never forget that conversation. "Hello ma'am, I called to tell you that I know where your car is." This was not what I'd been expecting to hear. "Where is it?" I asked. He gave a location and offered me his phone number in case I had any questions. The whole exchange was strange, but I took his number then hung up. I ran downstairs to Phillip and told him about the call. Phillip hurriedly put on his boots as he shouted, "Where is it?" I said, "The man kept hesitating to give me the info, like he wanted a reward or something." (I found out soon that he didn't want a reward, he had a story to tell!) I gave Phillip the address Robert had given me and he left. I then called Phillip and told him to be careful and that I was sending the police to the location. The police arrived, checked the VIN# and said that it was not my car. How weird it all was didn't kick in right away, but I thought; *a month or so has passed since the initial car theft, so why is Phillip still super angry, irritated and walking around with a fixed scowl on his face?* Days passed and Phillip got more creative with his fabricated stories; this time in response to why he changed the house locks, he said, "I let the guy who hung out at my evening job stay the night. I fell asleep and he took the keys and car, and that's why I had the locks changed." (Lie#2)

Okay, so now I have heard two myths so far and it made me wonder, *what's behind door or lie number 3?* That day I went to work and was asked to stay late and I initially agreed to do so. But I couldn't stop thinking about all the foolishness going on, so during my lunch break, I called Mr. Robert. I can still quote verbatim the conversation I had with him. I said, "Hello, this is the lady you called about the car." He responded, "Yeah, Blue has your car. She took me to the store and I found some checks and stuff in it with your name and phone number on it." I said, "Blue? Sir, I don't know you or Blue!"

Mr. Robert replied, "Ma'am I know you, but you don't know me; you not from here, you from New Orleans, you went home to see your people. I know Blue from around the way." (Blue was a known streetwalker). Blue shared details with Mr. Robert about a fool she propositioned and hung out with him for a night or two or three. Blue also shared the details about Phillip's wife (me) being out of town per Phillip! (I guess Phillip felt the need to share my whereabouts with his house guest so she would be more relaxed and comfortable with what was about to take place in my bed and in my home). A wise man one once said "Not even a dog poops where he sleeps."

"She'd been hanging out with your husband for some days." Mr. Robert was pouring the tea! "Blue had been staying over your house and when your husband fell asleep, she took your car." Phillip should have known when you lay down with dogs you get flees. I felt like I couldn't breathe; but I kept listening. Mr. Robert continued with how he felt the need to tell me because, "Blue is writing checks and ordering "a-lot-a-stuff." Not only was I subjected to the sacrilegious behavior(s) Phillip had inflicted on me and my children; I'd also have to deal with identity theft, fraud, credit disputes, credit report(s) and the list goes on. I felt contamination brought on by this person I called my "husband."

Mr. Robert then said, "take care of yourself Miss," and hung up. I'd heard enough and I wasn't only livid, but afraid for myself and my children. Heart beating fast now, I ran back to work, grabbed my purse and keys, and told my manager I wouldn't be able to work late due to a family emergency. I was already haunted by what happened to the poor woman in our neighborhood who'd been recently murdered by her husband. All I could think about now was racing home before Lori and P.J. got there from school. I was afraid for myself and my children at this point. People knew things about me, my children, our whereabouts and movements and all I had to go on were the lies Phillip was telling.

Mr. Robert disclosed information that I thought only Phillip and my family were privy to. I didn't go to work the next day. I didn't feel well and P.J. had contracted "pink eye." I called Phillip and asked him to leave work early to take P.J. to the doctor. I was also ready to CONFRONT HIM. Once

Phillip arrived I asked him, "Who is this floozy named Blue and what the hell happened with my car?" He shouted "I told you the truth but you're looking for the dirt!" I said, "NO! The dirt is in the truth and this is what happens when you go out hunting for sex with a moral-less creature and it's obvious your moral compass registered zero when you decided to bring a floozy into our home!"

I then told Phillip that the police dispatcher had given me a number for the officer handling the case if I had any questions or concerns. In response Phillip yelled, "Well call him then!" I dialed the number then and there, and Officer Sergeant, who had never answered before, picked up! I shared my early morning phone call from Mr. Robert with him along with my concerns. By now Phillip was looking very nervous!

"Where's your husband now?" The officer asked. I answered, "He's here anxiously following me around the house." Officer Sergeant said, "Put him on the phone." I gave Phillip the phone and he went downstairs and stepped outside on to the patio. I stood in the doorway watching him. I could literally see the muscles jumping around Phillip's face. I ran upstairs to grab the other phone and caught the end of their conversation. Officer Sergeant told Phillip, "You need to call me back as soon as you can talk, and if I find out you're lying and you falsified your initial report, you'll have bigger problems!" Phillip hung up and left to take P.J. to the pediatrician. So I called him on his cell. When he picked up I said, "If you never listened to anything I've ever said before, HERE ME NOW! That officer is giving you a chance to redeem yourself as a man and if you keep lying to him, he's going to "slam" you and you'll lose big time!" Then I paused and said, "I HAVE ONE QUESTION FOR YOU PHILLIP: "DID YOU USE A CONDOM?" There was a long pause then he said, "Yes."

I hung up the phone, but was a barrel of tears. I became Wonder Woman strong and lifted my California King bed and threw it down the stairs and out the front door. My neighbor happened to be outside and asked, "You need any help?" My response—"Thanks, but I got it from here."

This shameful event came full circle and the police department contacted me and asked if I would meet them at the recovery site to identify the car. This time the VIN# was a match. The car was recovered and ended up back in front of our home. I came to the conclusion that the man I loved, the man

I called my "Snickerdoodle" preferred strumpets, as some men do over his wife. A strumpet as defined by Merriam Webster as a female prostitute or a promiscuous woman. At that moment, I realized that I had married "The Despicable One." Once the truth came out and Phillip was nakedly exposed. I told him, "I'm a child of the King and he protects me and my children from strangers and potential danger! I had to make life-changing decisions like to leave my husband and move on with my life; Phillip's behavior was just that—"Despicable." My son P.J. was still in primary school and sometimes he would run around the house randomly yelling "Where my momma keys?" And I would just laugh

Yes! (In my singing voice.) I can laugh now because I received beauty for my ashes. I've moved on now and my blessings may have been delayed but they weren't denied.

Wishing God's blessings upon us all!.

ABOUT

Deloris "DJ" Strahan

Deloris is a mother, Grandmother, serial entrepreneur, travel agent and widower and health and wellness coach who is on a journey to reinvent, reset, and reclaim her life's dream, which has been put on a shelf for a very long time. She has a certification in Christian counselor and works with teens in her church during the summer. After her husband passed in 2007, she began to reach out to many women both on and offline who needed someone to talk to. She realized that there are so many people in the world who were suffering from the same issues she had been suffering from. As a result she created a small group called My Sisters Kompany and Me, which she operates out of her home, where people meet in person or by phone. Many people have reached out to Deloris because of the information they've seen on her Facebook page where she shares positive messages every day. Her ultimate goal is to connect with widows all over the world.

Deloris has said that, "At this time in my life I don't know how far I will go with my message, but I pray that it will touch at least one person. And while I don't have many accolades to brag about or a long resume, what I know for sure is that I am a woman who loves and cares for people. I've also carried a dream all my life and believe that it's never too late to take the testimony of a dreamer and make it a reality."

Find Deloris here:

Website: www.delstrahan.com
Email: darcauswings@aol.com
Facebook: Deloris.strahan
Instagram: augustmoon45
Twitter: @augustsky46
Phone: 832-284-5176

TESTIMONY OF A DREAMER

By Deloris (DJ) Strahan

*So be strong and courageous! Do not be afraid
and do not panic before them, for the lord your
God will personally go ahead of you. He will
neither fail you nor abandon you.*

— Deuteronomy 31:6

As a child I had a lot of dreams about the kind of life that I wanted for myself
and how I wanted my life to be. I was raised in the fifties and sixties. I didn't
know much about life back then. But what I did know was that you did what
you were told to do and you didn't break the rules. As the oldest child in my
family, I was given a lot of responsibility, especially at a young age. I was
taught early on how to do laundry as well as how to cook and clean. When I
think about it, I was put in charge of everything, including taking care of my
sisters and my brother.

My mom was a single parent who did her best to raise us. She held down two
jobs and worked both day and night. As the oldest I was expected to make
sure things went well at home. I never liked being in this position because if
anything ever went wrong, I'd get blamed for it. And trust me, things went
wrong a lot. I would often get whippings for things that my brother and
sisters did because I was in charge of them. They never listened to me. They
did whatever they wanted to do most of the time, and then they'd have the
nerve to laugh about it and tease me by saying, "You're gonna catch it!" I
knew exactly what that meant. I was afraid of getting a whipping because

in those days black kids were whipped with extensions cords or homemade switches from the yard. Black folks don't talk about it often and when we do, we usually laugh about it. But truth be told, black folks would beat the crap out of their children.

I guess you could call me a woman-child because I was robbed of child-like things. I didn't have birthday parties nor did I get to play much like my sisters and brother because most of the time I was busy doing chores. I was a lonely kid who kept to herself. As I think about it now, this is when the dreams began. Since I was alone most of the time with no one to talk to I started keeping a diary. We never had much money, but every now and then we had family friends who would give us a few bucks. I'd save mine inside a baking powder can, until I had enough to buy myself a diary. I actually bought two. I don't remember the price of them, all I remember is having enough to buy two of them. This is when my journey inside of my head made its way to paper. I wrote every day about what was going on in my life and about things that happened to me. I wrote about what I liked and what I didn't like. One thing I hated was all the moving. We moved so much that I couldn't even keep count. I never understood this and back then you didn't ask questions. When we moved to Texas, as the years went by, I wrote in my diary that when I grew up, I wouldn't move so much. I have truly kept that promise because today, some forty plus years later, I still live in Texas.

Growing up in Texas was okay. I always knew that I was different from my brother and sisters. I would often see myself in a different place and time. I didn't talk much and I kept my feelings inside. I didn't consider myself cute or pretty. I was very skinny and didn't feel like there was anything special about me. Most girls had better shaped bodies than mine. During gym class, I hated dressing in front of the other girls and having to take showers. Because like in the movie, *Carrie*, when the mother said, "they're going to laugh at you," those kids laughed at me many times. They called me bony, and many nights I would lie in bed, crying myself to sleep. This is when I would really focus on my dream of one day becoming someone great. I didn't know how I was going to do it, but I was determined and knew that God had a special calling on my life.

As harsh as things were, they were bearable until I turned fourteen and was molested by the man that my mother had married. I never told anyone in my family about it because as I said before, back then kids my age were seen but not heard. The first time he attacked me was late one night after closing his soda shop where I worked after school. After I finished cleaning the bathroom in the back, he walked over to me and tried to kiss me. I pushed him away and said, "What are you doing?" I tried to get away from him, but he was bigger and taller than me. I only weighed about ninety pounds, but I fought as he pushed me down on the couch that was in the back. I screamed, "Leave me alone! Please stop it!" I was scared and crying as he held me down putting his hand over my mouth. He kept saying, "I am not going to hurt you. Stop fighting me." But I still fought for my life yet nothing stopped him. This evil man raped me and he was not even sorry about what he'd done. He went back to being normal, as if nothing ever happen.

I didn't tell anyone about it because he threatened me. At that point I felt destroyed and ashamed. I was so confused, my emotions ran the gamut from being guilty to not really understanding what had happened to me. He stole my life at that moment. I wanted to die. I was hurting so bad. It was disgusting and it changed who I was from that moment on.

What happened to me should never happen to any young girl. I thought it was over that one time and I could go ahead with my life or at least what was left of it, and try to forget about it. Three months passed and here I was thinking that I was safe. But because my mother sometimes worked at night it left me open for it to happen again. He would always look at me in strange ways. And back then my sister and I slept in the same bed, but one night she wasn't home. My brother and baby sister was there but asleep. I was in bed sleeping when he came into the room, got into my bed, put his hand over my mouth and told me don't scream. He said that if I did he would hurt me and if I told anyone he was going to make it very hard for my mother. He was a mean man. He held me down and raped me again. I cried and did what I could to fight him off. I even bit him, but nothing stopped him. I was praying that my mother would come home and catch him. But she didn't.

I cried all day and the next day. I was damaged for life. I felt sick and dirty. I was also ashamed. I prayed to God, asking him what I could have done wrong for this to happen to me. I felt so low and less than a human being. I carried this feeling all throughout my adolescent life. He attempted to rape me many times after that, but I made up my mind that I was going to fight him with all I had or die trying if he came near me again. My mother and my Grandmothers used to have these big butcher knives. One day, I took one from my Grandmother's house without her knowing it. I placed it under my pillow every night and if he ever came back I vowed that I was going to hurt him really bad just like he'd hurt me.

About two weeks later when my mother was at work, he tried it again and I hate to say this but I cut him on his arm. I don't know how bad it was and I didn't care. I was not going to let him rape me again. After that, he never tried to touch me again. But I had been praying that God would find a way to get me out of that mess. I prayed he would die from the wound I gave him. I heard that the cut was very bad, or that my mother would question him and to try to find out the truth, but of course he lied and said that he got hurt at work.

My brother and sisters didn't liked him from the start. We never understood why our mom married him. I wanted to leave home, but I was so young and didn't have anywhere to go. But God stepped in when my Grandmother asked me to come and stay with her for a while. I still suffered for a long time because of what happen to me. I'd have nightmares, and would wake up screaming. I even stop talking at one point. My Grandmother would ask what was wrong, but I never told her because they probably would have killed him for harming me.

I survived this ordeal and life went on for me. I prayed a lot but I was never fully healed from my inner pain or struggles because the damage was done. I had to find a way to forget it, but I couldn't. I just made do with the cards I was dealt. I started to really dislike myself for being a young girl. I tried so many ways to make myself look unattractive because there were other rape attempts from men who were supposed to be friends and uncles of the family. My mom eventually got divorced. I'm not sure why and I really didn't care. All I knew was that I was finally free. My prayers were delayed but they were not denied.

I was only sixteen years old when I met James Strahan. We were in high school. He was a nice boy who was always respectable and treated me special. He was tall and well mannered. We started dating and the rest is history. He was my knight who came to save me from all that I was going though. He knew my story because I shared it with him. He told me from day one, that I would never have to go through anything like that again as long as he was in my life. He was my protector. We got married a year out of high school. I was a young bride full of passion and dreams of being someone great one day despite the many things that happened to me, which were beyond my control.

I believe that God stepped in and saved me by bringing James into my life. I was still mad at my dad for not being in my life to save me. My husband and I talked many times about meeting up with him. James actually made it happen. I was twenty-six years old with two children when I took my first plane ride to visit my dad in Michigan. I was scared and full of nerves. I flew alone. My family didn't go with me. James wanted me to spend that time with him by myself and so I did. I arrived safely but since my father hadn't seen me as an adult he didn't know me. They were waiting for me with a sign with my name on it. So I decide to play a little trick by asking them if they were waiting on someone because most of the people had passed through already. They stood there looking puzzled as I walked away. I waited for a few more minutes before walking back over to them. Then I said, "Hello dad and mom, it's me!"

They were so excited to see me. They hugged me so much and talked about what an attractive young lady I had grown up to be. My dad was such a cool guy. He was very handsome and quite a charmer. I saw firsthand why he might be liked by the ladies. I spent two weeks with them getting to know him and allowing him to get to know me. Then the time came for me to go back home. I loved that summer. It was a dream come true. Once again, it was a delayed reunion, but I was so glad that I had not been denied that moment.

Things were great for the next forty or so years until my best friend and lover, my dear husband passed away suddenly. It was devastating. I was totally unprepared for what was to come. After the service, when the music stopped and everyone had gone home, I went through many lows. I had many sleepless nights, crying spells and times of not feeling anything at all.

He was a great man and an awesome father. I actually lived in denial for two years that he was gone. It took me a long time to figure out how I was going to make in the world without my protector. I was afraid to go outside and step out into the unknown. But one day after sitting on the floor crying I decided that I was sick of it. I asked God to show me a way out of the darkness. This is when the light appeared in my head and God spoke to me and said, "Remember that dream I gave you, get back up and go after it." I had some reservations, but as time went on I got up and started moving toward my dreams. I've always had lots of hobbies and I love cooking, sewing, and making gift baskets. I also love working with people at my church and found myself motivating others. I had found my voice. I am now on my way to moving forward. I am living my life as an example for people who are struggling and believe that there is no hope for tomorrow. I am a testimony to the fact that there is light at the end of the tunnel and living proof that all things are possible with God.

I am Deloris J. Strahan and I dedicate this chapter to my late husband James W. Strahan.

Stay blessed and remember…

Therefore I tell you. Whatever you ask for in prayer,
Believe that you have received it, it will be yours. — Mark 11:24.

ABOUT

Jennifer Halstead

Jennifer Halstead is a tax accountant who also teaches high school math in Southern California. As part of the school's Tech-know Team, she is enthusiastic about using technology to teach in her classroom. She has helped shape the curriculum in the school district and is a Common Core Lead Teacher. Passionate about her students' overall education, she founded Mathletes, a program to engage and excite them about math outside the classroom, she organizes field trips to visit NASA and to ballet performances, she administers the school tutoring program and is the sophomore class advisor.

She has been awarded the Teacher of the Year, received a Crystal Apple Award for Outstanding Teachers and is a yearly winner of the school's Teacher Spirit award.

Jennifer has a B.S. in Business and Accounting, an M.A. in Secondary Teaching, and a Ph.D. in Education. She has a mathematics credential and holds certificates in Teaching Advanced Placement and Tax Preparation.

Jennifer has two sons, one now working in Las Vegas, while the other is still in college. An avid reader, she is a member her local book club, loves anything Disney, holds season tickets to the theater, and travels whenever she can.

Email:	jen_jen23@hotmail.com
Twitter:	@Jhalstead604
Linkedin:	jennifer-pettit-halstead-28048060/

ROLLER COASTER OF LIFE

By Jennifer Halstead

I was eighteen and barely out of high school when I got married and had my first baby. I knew it would be tough, and I didn't know many people who had marriages that lasted, but he said he loved me and I believed in fairy tales. I married him, uprooted my life in Las Vegas and followed him to Texas. By the time I was pregnant with my second child two years later, the stress of surviving had taken its toll on our marriage and we separated. I went back to Vegas.

When I gave birth, I expected him to come immediately to see his new child, but it took him six months and losing his job to do it. Finally though, he moved back to Las Vegas and we agreed to fix our marriage. We got an apartment and he got a job. I was naive enough to believe that things were going to work out. I had enrolled in the local community college, he had a job that paid well in construction, and we attended church on Sundays as a family. The boys were both happy and healthy. Life was good again.

I still vividly remember the day everything changed. My husband ran me a bubble bath and gave me a glass of wine. He told me to have some relaxing "me time" while he played with the boys. When I was done, I came out to the living room to sit with my family. He told me that his best friend, Scott, was waiting outside. He had just broken up with his girlfriend and needed to talk. They might drive around for a bit while they talked. Since they were going to be out, I asked him to pick up some milk on the way back. The babies would need it in the morning. He agreed, gave me a quick kiss on the cheek and walked out the door.

Scott had a cell phone, a luxury that we couldn't afford at the time. When they weren't back by the time I put the boys to bed, I called and spoke to my husband. He said they were still driving around, they'll remember the milk, and he'll be home soon. I went to bed. The next morning, I woke up as the children were getting up. I went to the kitchen to make breakfast, and there was no milk. Annoyed, I started looking for my husband. When I discovered he wasn't home, I called Scott. My call was sent to voicemail. I called a few of our friends, all with no answer. Worried, I even called a few hospitals to see if either of them had been admitted. When there was no news, I figured I should just get ready for the day. As soon as I opened the closet, I knew. All of his clothes were missing! I started frantically searching the room to see what else was gone. My jewelry was gone, including the wedding band that I had removed the night before for my bath.

I was twenty-two, had two babies, and my husband had just walked out on us. Day care was expensive, so I had been staying home to care for the boys and had no job. He had left right before the end of the month, meaning in a few days the rent and bills would be due. We had very little food left. Since his payday was the next day, I called his boss to see if I could pick up his check. His boss told me my husband had already gotten it when he quit a few days prior. He must have been planning this for a while. I was devastated, furious, and confused. What saved me was that I had been babysitting a friend's child for extra cash, and had been stashing the money away into savings. That money was all I had, and it wasn't much.

I didn't quite have enough to get us through the month, so I had to do something quickly. There were programs that were designed to get people in my situation back on their feet. My kids came first, and they needed food and a place to live. I went to the welfare office and applied. They approved me for emergency food stamps and cash aide. I went to the housing office and was placed on a waiting list. It wasn't much but it would help. I applied for jobs everywhere I could over the next few days. A Home-Town Buffet was opening soon on the corner by our apartment, and I managed to get hired as a cashier. During the interview, they asked if I was on welfare, which I thought strange. But I got hired anyway. I was a "welfare hire" meaning the state paid Home-Town for hiring me through the Welfare to Work program. It wasn't full time, but twenty to thirty hours a week at the minimum wage of $5.10 an hour was better than nothing. This allowed me to have time to continue taking classes at the college. For the first time, I put my kids in day care. This was also subsidized by the state.

It was difficult to go from spending the majority of my time with my boys, to leaving them with other people. Their grandparents on both sides helped out with watching the kids while I was in school, and they went to day care while I worked. I tried to make up for being away by playing with them as much as I could when I was home. His parents, ironically, were my lifesavers. They bought the boys clothes whenever they needed it.

I continued going to the church every Sunday, and bible study on Wednesdays when I could. The church community was a constant source of compassion and friendship for me and the boys. At Christmas, the church brought a box of food, some presents for the boys and a check for me. I never thought my life would come to this but I was grateful for the blessings I had. I don't know how I would have made it through those times without the generosity and support of the church.

A few months later, my name came up on the waitlist for housing. It was for an apartment in a state-owned housing development in a rough area of town. The rent was $42 a month. When your name comes up for these things, you have two choices: accept what is offered or turn it down and start over from square one. Money was so tight, I was barely getting by, so I took it. A few days later, I moved my kids to an area that was referred to as "crack alley."

The complex was painted pink. There were two rows of apartments, with a parking lot between them. Along each row, there were groups of apartments surrounding a courtyard. Some courtyards had playground equipment, some had benches. My courtyard was a dirt square. My unit was the bottom corner, and had two bedrooms. The kitchen was large enough for a small table to make it a dining area too. I bought a round white plastic outdoor table and covered it with a tablecloth. I did what I could to make it look like "home."

The first day in the house, I unpacked our small amount of belongings and put the boys to bed. The bedroom windows faced the street, while the living room and kitchen faced the courtyard. You heard cars and people out on the street when you were in either bedroom. Lying in my bed, I tried to get used to the unfamiliar sounds when suddenly, there was a rattling at the window. A large, dark figure startled me and was staring into my room from the window. "Go away!" I yelled and closed the blinds. A few minutes later there was banging on the door. "Open up, let me in, Tara!" I was terrified and yelled back "there's no Tara here! Go away!" I have no idea if it was the same person or a different one, but he kept banging on the door and yelling with his booming voice to open the door. I was so glad I had locked the deadbolt. While he continued to scream behind the door, I went to my side of the door and continued to yell back, "There's no Tara here! Go away or I'm calling the cops!" I don't know how long this went on, probably just a minute or two, but it felt like eternity. That night, and several others after that, I slept on the couch with a baseball bat in my hand.

There were three neighbors in the complex who were also single mothers. Selena lived above me, Mary was across from my unit, and Alex was in the unit above Mary's. They each had one child and we would gather in the courtyard to let our children play together. Mary, whose son was the oldest, around four or five, mostly kept to herself, was usually quiet and preferred to stay inside. On the other hand, Alex and Selena were outgoing and energetic and they accepted me instantly. Alex's daughter was about two, and Selena's wasn't quite one yet. My boys were one and three by then. Our children enjoyed playing together and we would talk while the kids played. I was the only one going to school, Alex had a job and Selena stayed home with her daughter.

There are things about living in poverty that you don't really think about until you're in it. Things like making a choice between eating dinner and putting gas in the car to get to work, or choosing between paying the electric bill or paying to do the laundry. Selena had grown up in government housing and knew the ropes. She was the one who taught me how to make some of those choices, and how to get around others. She told me that the 7-Eleven behind our apartment building took food stamps. We would walk there with the kids a few times a week to get Slurpees. She also showed me the meal room, where the state subsidized a breakfast and lunch program for the children. It was right next to the police annex at the end of the complex. Breakfast was year round, but lunch was only during breaks from school and weekends. The food was only for the kids and we went almost daily. We learned that they threw away the uneaten food afterward. When I made friends with the lady who ran the program she would let us take home any leftovers if we came at the end. You can bet we tried to come at the end of every meal time. By doing this, I was able to stretch my food budget.

Once a month, we would go to the food bank and get a box containing oatmeal, cheese, and canned vegetables. At a nearby grocery outlet, macaroni was 0.25 cents a box, which was a staple in our house. They also sold a ten pound pack of hamburger meat for less than $5, and I would get one of those and cut it into twelve packages. Each was slightly less than a pound. Many meals were made with macaroni and hamburger meat during that time. I made sure my children were always fed, and they never went hungry, even if I had to skip a meal or two along the way. When I had to skip dinner, I would go to bed early because when you're sleeping, you don't know you're hungry. Working at Home-Town Buffet, I got free meals when I worked, so I made sure to eat a big meal on those days.

The complex had a laundry room, and it cost about $2.50 to wash and dry a load of clothes. When you need to choose between paying for electricity or putting that money in a washing machine and dryer, having electricity wins every time. Selena taught me how to wash in the bathtub. I would give the boys a bath, and then add more soap to the water when they were done. Once all of the clothes were in the tub, I would step into it and walk around kicking my feet on the clothes or I would let the boys splash and kick to agitate it. After a few minutes, I rinsed each piece, then wrung them out before hanging them. Since I didn't trust leaving my clothes outside for fear they'd be stolen, I would hang them to dry around the house. It would sometimes take a full day and night for the clothes to dry. There was almost always clothes hanging from doorways in the house. It saved money, and I didn't have to drag my clothes across the complex.

Though I lived in "crack alley," I never really expected to have to know how to avoid getting attacked. I'm grateful that Alex taught me how to do this. Her advice was that if it was just one guy, simply start acting crazy; get loud and wild when he started to approach. If it was more than one guy, you needed to start scratching your privates and say things like, "oh yeah! It's been too long!" If you act like you want it, they'll go away. We must have been an interesting sight, practicing as we walked to and from 7-Eleven! Although, she did say you'd have to fight if it didn't work. I carried mace on my keychain. Most of the time, simply crossing the street or walking the other way when I was uncomfortable was all it took to avoid trouble. There were only a few occasions where I had to pull out the mace, but I never had to actually use it.

There were good times, like when Alex, Selena and I could share a babysitter and the three of us would go out to the nearby bar pretending we were just normal, single, twenty-two year olds out to have some fun. We would listen to the bands, dance, and have a few drinks. There were also bad times, like when they cut my hours at the buffet or when my boss kept harassing me. I went through a serious depression for several weeks. During that time, my house, my kids, and I were all dirty. I felt hopeless and thought that the struggle was pointless. Every time I thought we were doing better, something would happen to knock us back down. When I used food stamps at the store, people would look in my cart to see what "their tax dollars" were paying for. They told me to my face to stop being lazy and just get a job. A few times, I was told I was worthless and lacking as a human being. And, even though I knew it wasn't true, what they said hurt and it still affects me. But deep down I knew that I had to stay positive, and believe that this was merely a temporary situation. Things had to get better, and dwelling on the negative just makes everything worse. I had my two kids to think about and I had to make their life better. They deserved so much more than they were getting.

So I worked hard and fought to get my kids and myself into a better life. I went to school to get my degree, worked as many hours as I could get at the buffet, and spent as much time as I could enjoying my children. Having them was what got me through those tough times. We had play group at the library, and played in the park or in the courtyard every day. For a special treat, we would walk to the 7-Eleven and get Slurpees, or for fun, go across the street to the mall to window shop. We would play with the puppies in the pet store and I would promise them that one day, when we have a real house, with a yard, they could have their own puppy. We'd also go to the toy store and they'd play with the display toys as long as they wanted to.

While it wasn't the most ideal situation, and was downright terrifying at times, that time in my life taught me a lot. It taught me to be tough, and to let go of any preconceived notions that I had about people and even myself. I lived in those apartments for just under two years. Mary eventually moved. Alex got a boyfriend, and he moved her to Arizona. Selena got a boyfriend, and had another baby. When I finished my associate's degree at the community college, I took a position at my father's accounting business in California and moved away. I tried to keep in touch but our lives were busy. Eventually, phone numbers were disconnected and we lost contact.

The boys' father showed up about six months after we moved into the pink apartments. I found out that he had left me to live with his girlfriend. I told him I wanted a divorce, and made sure that he knew I didn't care who he was seeing, but I wanted him to be involved in the boys' lives. A few weeks later, he stopped coming to visit again. He would continue to be in and out of their lives over the next few years. About once or twice a year, he would call and get them excited about a visit that never took place. Being a child of divorce myself, I was against badmouthing him to them. I made excuses for him when his promises didn't come through. When the boys were in middle school, they actually did go for a week two summers in a row. After that he just kind of disappeared again. Being so close to his parents I knew he was alive, and periodically heard a little about what he was doing. But that was about it. My youngest boy didn't really seem bothered by it, he never really knew his dad. However the oldest always claimed to remember when his dad was around, and missed him a great deal.

I stayed focused on my education and getting us to a better place. It was a hard road, working full time, going to school, and raising the boys on my own. I had some family in the area where I moved, so they were of some help. My children and I moved twelve times over the next ten years, each to a slightly better apartment as my job situation improved. Once I had my bachelor's degree I decided that "cubical work" was not for me. I had made friends who were teachers and they encouraged me to get my subbing credential to see if I liked teaching. It turned out that I loved teaching. I continued going to school, and got my master's degree at the same time as my teaching credential, and became a high school math teacher. I bought a house and settled down in the community. The boys were active, so I put them in soccer, karate, football, and baseball. I always managed to be the team manager or coach so I could stay involved in what they were doing. I kept going to school and taking classes, trying to instill education as a priority with my kids. My children are now both out of high school and doing well and I am at peace. All of which may have been delayed but certainly wasn't denied.

—— ABOUT ——

Toni Coleman Brown

Toni Coleman Brown is an author, coach, marketing expert, and motivational speaker. She is also the CEO and Founder of the Network for Women in Business, an online community for women business owners who seek affordable cutting-edge training and the ability to connect and advance with other like-minded individuals. The motto for the Network is, "We EDUCATE to ELEVATE women in business." Toni is also the host and creator of The Small Business Bootcamp for Women and the Online Marketing Mastermind Live events.

Toni has been featured in the *New York Amsterdam News*, the *Network Journal Magazine, Our Time Newspaper*, Black Enterprise Online, *Working Woman Magazine* and WPIX 11's Working Woman Report. She is the author of *Quantum Leap: How to Make a Quantum Leap in Your Network Marketing Business* and the compiler and co-author of *Network to Increase Your Net Worth* and *Delayed But Not Denied: 20 Inspirational Stories of Life and Resiliency.*

Toni is on a mission to fulfill her God-ordained purpose of changing the lives of millions. Toni lives in Queens, New York with her husband and two daughters.

Toni can be reached at:

Email: toni@networkforwomeninbusiness.com

Websites: www.networkforwomeninbusiness.com
                      www.tonicolemanbrown.com
                      www.smallbusinessbootcampforwomen.com
                      www.onlinemarketingmastermindlive.com

Facebook: tonicolemanbrown

Twitter   @tonibrown

Instagram: tonicolemanbrown

TRUSTING GOD TO LEAD THE WAY

by Toni Coleman Brown

Many years ago, when I first began to call myself a life changer I never knew that I would be responsible for positively impacting the lives of so many young people. But in my role as the Director of the Internship program for the largest transportation outlet in the U.S., I am able to do just that—change lives. From the confused student who doesn't know what he or she wants to do after they graduate high school or college, to the full-time employee who would like to get some direction regarding their next career move, I'm helping them all. Nothing gives me more joy than placing a student in an area that ends up landing them a full-time opportunity or facilitating a workshop and seeing the lightbulbs go off in their eyes showing that they actually, "Get it." Yes. I actually get paid to do what I love and I landed in a place where I get to utilize all of my coaching, training, and mentoring skills in a way that's making a difference in the lives of others. The past three years have been some of the best years of my life. It took a long time to get here, but I'm glad that I did.

Looking back I can say that it's easy to go through life comparing yourself to others. We all have goals and dreams. We would all like to achieve everything our heart desires. As a little girl I dreamed of a life with a nice house, a car, wonderful kids and a loving and supportive husband. I dreamed of having a career that I absolutely loved. I never really wanted fame or to be famous because I wanted to be able to live my life on my own terms, not having to worry about hiding from the public. I didn't quite know what road would lead me to that corner office or that "perfect" lifestyle and I never really had anyone in particular to guide me. All I knew was that I would never stop trying or never stop seeking. I would never give up.

Growing up in Louisiana was interesting. We never had, what I like to say was a lot, in terms of riches, but we never went without. Or if we did it really wasn't that obvious to me. During my last year of high school, I was blessed to participate in a co-op program that allowed me to go to school for a few hours in the morning and work in an office for the remainder of the day. I was lucky enough to land a gig working in the Human Resources department of a local bank. I really enjoyed myself. I loved my boss. She was a German lady who spoke broken English and was married to a black man who drove the streetcar down St. Charles Avenue. She had met him while he was in the Army stationed in Germany. Even though it was the 80's, we were still living in the Deep South. My boss, Angelika got a kick out of hopping on the streetcar that her husband drove and giving him a big kiss, to piss everyone off. I learned so much from her. She was my first mentor. She turned me on to some bad habits too like drinking Gin and Tonic (Yes. You can drink at eighteen in Louisiana), but she also taught me everything she knew. Needless to say, when it was time for me to go off to college, they offered me a job and wanted me to stay. I graciously turned it down. I literally didn't know how much of a big deal that was until I look back on it now. They offered me a full-time position working in the Human Resources department of a bank when I was eighteen years old. I guess I was always mature for my age. But I never could see what others saw in me. I honestly still struggle with that today.

In the fall of 1984, I left that job and started college at Dillard University. It was not my school of choice, I wanted to go to Howard University, but because I had not taken the SAT, I couldn't attend Howard like I'd planned. But the following year, I successfully got myself together to attend Howard. I was so excited, but I was also so confused. I didn't know what I wanted to do. All I knew was that like most kids, my family said to me that I had two choices, either go to school or go to work and if I went to school, I better had majored in something that could land me a job. So I thought that engineering would be it. Plus my half-brother Lucky, whom I really admired was an engineer and I wanted to be like him.

I started Howard in the School of Engineering in 1985 and I was on my way. But Howard was different. It wasn't very nurturing like Dillard and most of the professors didn't speak English. Then to top it all off, the student population wasn't that nice or friendly. Walking across the yard at Howard was not like at Dillard. Most of the students at Dillard would at least speak, but the students at Howard... they would get close to you and turn their head. I was like a fish out of water. Nothing came easily to me. I felt so misguided and it was only through divine intervention, my mom's prayers, and a friendly personality that allowed me to make friends and find "angels" to help me along the way.

I didn't do well in the School of Engineering at all. I struggled hard until I finally decided to switch to the School of Business. When I look at my transcript today, it looks like a hot flaming mess, with the exception of that one summer when I got my act together, took six classes and got six A's. Thank God for that summer. At least it pulled up my GPA. In 1990, I finally graduated with a decent GPA and a BBA in Finance. I also was blessed to have a job. Yes. I had successfully interviewed both on campus and off campus in New York City at the Port Authority of NY & NJ. I landed a job as a Management Trainee in their Office of Management and Budget. So after six years of struggling to graduate from college the country girl found herself in the Big Apple. That was an amazing season in my life. One of my former roommates and best friend was from the Bronx, so I was able to crash with her and her family until I found a place in NJ I shared with a classmate.

New York City in the 90's was crazy fun. Quite a few of my former classmates were working for companies in the city. There was a crew of us from Howard and a few other HBCU's like Morehouse and Hampton we were constantly hanging out with. We had parties and surrounded ourselves with beautiful people. I got engaged to a fella I'd met at Howard and got un-engaged not long after I arrived in the City. I guess there was just too much temptation around me for that to last. I stayed at the Port Authority for about six years before I moved on. They were having layoffs and I didn't want to stay. I was still very confused about what I wanted to do. But I did get a Master's Degree in Creative Writing from City College during that time. Because the one thing that I always knew about myself was that I loved to write. Maybe a good mentor would have guided me to the School of Communications at Howard. But I was always insecure about myself and my looks and was too afraid to get in front of the camera back then. My love of books guided me to Bookspan where I worked on a special task force and helped the company develop Black Expressions, one of the first African-American book clubs. I was so proud of that book club. I helped to name it, I came up with its tag line, "Getting Connected Through Books" and I became the Marketing Director. I had a natural instinct for marketing. My career took off. I made a lot of money, had two children and picked up a husband or two during those years. But I was eventually laid off. That wasn't a problem for me though because I had really taken off in the home-business arena. I decided to stay home with my young children and work my home business. During this time, I reached the top of my home-business marketing plan and wrote my first book. But when the market got bad I knew I had to go back to work. I uploaded my resume on Monster and was quickly hired as a consultant for the MTA New York City Transit.

I hated working for NYC Transit when I first started. I prayed before I even started that I would work in Transit, but that I wouldn't become "of" Transit. But things changed for me when the Executive Vice President at the time hired me to be his Director. After working for him for three years I was able to get a clear view of the agency and I knew exactly where I wanted to be, Human Resources. Because someone was retiring, an opportunity to become the Director of the Internship Program opened up in HR. I jumped at it. I successfully interviewed and got the job.

Like I said before it's been almost three years now and I am in love with what I do. A few weeks ago I had two students come into my office and they had some questions, but it quickly became evident that they just wanted to talk. They came into my office in one state, which was kind of down, but they left uplifted. I felt like a superhero and was happy because this is all a part of my role. Today, I assist colleges with understanding the needs of employers by sitting on panels and hosting 1:1 conversations. I assist parents by providing resources related to giving their children the opportunity to gain access to work experience. And I provide students with the opportunity to earn while they learn. I'll be documenting my knowledge and experience by penning a new book very soon.

While I am living my life's mission by assisting in changing the lives of young people. I still find it ironic that more than thirty years when I was offered the opportunity to work in the Human Resources Department I turned it down. I often wonder where I would have been had I started out in HR from the beginning. I can only say that I may have been delayed, but I wasn't denied. I am going to continue to do what I believe God is calling for me to do and I'll continue to trust that he will order my steps.

---------- ABOUT ----------

Julia D. Shaw

Julia D. Shaw is a business professional with over twenty years of experience provides traditional and non-traditional consultation services assisting businesses. Her latest business venture is the Collaborative Experience, Inc. a life purpose partnership with Toni Coleman Brown, creating the joint venture book series *Delayed But Not Denied* and other enrichment events, workshops and experience. Their first compilation is *Delayed But Not Denied: 20 Inspirational Stories About Life and Resiliency*. Shaw is an emerging artist, a contributing author to the Amazon Bestseller, *Network to Increase Your Net Worth*, by Toni Coleman Brown and was featured in *Steppin' Out with Attitude: Sister, Sell your Dream*, by Anita Bunkley.

Shaw other business endeavors include, Lead Consultant at Shaw Biz Consulting (SBC) and True Joy Enterprises. Her insight has proven beneficial to entrepreneurs, small businesses, publishers, authors, corporations, radio stations, educational institutions, and nonprofit organizations.

For the last 20 years, Shaw continues to consult with the *Network Journal Magazine's* 40 Under Forty Achievement Awards and the 25 Influential Women in Business Awards and worked several years with, the National Black Writer's Conference coordinated by The Center of Black Literature at Medgar Evers College .

Shaw and/or her clients have been featured in New York Amsterdam News, New York Daily News, The New York Times, USA Today, the Network Journal Magazine, Black Enterprise Magazine among a host of newspapers, blogs/websites, TV and radio shows.

Julia is the proud mother of two daughters with three grandchildren, she lives in Queens, NY.

Websites:	www.delayedbutnotdenied.info
	www.shawbizconsulting.com
Email:	collaborativeexperience@gmail.com
LinkedIn:	julia_d_shaw1
Facebook:	juliadshaw1
	meettheauthorexperience
Twitter;	@juliadshaw1

MY SHIFT: I AM SELF-FOCUSED!

By Julia D. Shaw

We all have a story to tell.... Many of us have been placed in situations that were unfair and caused great pain. Life altering drama and trauma has left us feeling like the odds were stacked against us and we would never achieve success. Some scenarios we had very little control, "victims of circumstance." In other instances, the blame for undesirable results could be placed solely on our choices and decisions.

The most powerful catalysts to impact my life, resulting in positive growth and lasting change has been emotional pain and/or inner discomfort. It did not matter if this inner turmoil was due to a relationship, friendship, family, workplace, or in the business arena. You name the drama and I had it. Leave that man, he is abusive; she's not your friend, she slept with your man; she's your family and stole your jewelry; your job is not your passion or purpose, but it pays the bills; you finished the project but you have to chase your client for your final payment. Discomfort gave me the strength to shift my life in a different direction, to make a change. I like others have gone through a host of trials and tribulations, some seemed insurmountable. In retrospect, some situations were bigger in my mind than they actually were in reality.

I realized that I was the common denominator in all my life sagas and if it wasn't for uncomfortable experiences forcing me to take control in my life, I wouldn't be the person I am today.

The truth is I became sick and tired of doing the same thing and expecting different results. I was taking one step forward and two steps back... dancing in place to the same tune. Sometimes God has a way of looking out for us even when we don't know better... His message often is simple: move on or suffer!

149

My self-esteem was beaten down as a child and it definitely impacted my choices as an adult. Growing up I was a chubby, little light-skinned girl with glasses. I was teased to no end. "Point Dexter," "Oriental," "Fatso," and "Oreo" were the words that were used to chip away at the self-esteem my Momma worked so hard to instill in me. Growing up the light skin/dark skin colorism issues, caused me a great deal of emotional distress that stayed around well into my adulthood. I got to a point in my life when, I had to say to myself and anyone else who expressed THEIR issue with the color of my skin, "This is how God made me, I did not select my skin color. If you have an issue, it's your problem not mine." I refused to internalize *their* problems.

In my late 20's, I didn't know the power and importance of self-love. So, if I didn't love myself how could I expect anyone else to? During this time, while I was still in college and going through a rough relationship, I felt like I didn't have a friend in the world. One day while standing on the subway platform I ran into James, a classmate. I must've been looking sadder than sad because he asked me what was wrong. I told him all the things that were being done to me by the man who said he loved me. James said, "I'm going to tell you the secret to life." Then in a cool firm tone James said, "No one does anything to you that you don't allow them to do." His words stopped me in my tracks and I became angry and confused. "So, you're saying that I am responsible and what I'm going through all is my fault?" I refused to accept this truth and immediately dismissed it. Years passed and I finally realized this truth and applied it to my life. James was right and it was a hard pill to swallow. It took a lot of reflection for me to take responsibility and acknowledge that I had allowed negativity from others to impact my life, dictate my actions and create feelings of self-doubt. That in turn caused me to put myself into unhealthy situations.

My goal is to be the best I can be, to reshape my life and shift my energy. I work daily to change my inner voice, and aggressively reinvent my views of myself and others. I have come to terms with the mistakes I've made. It took years to release the anger and resentment I had been holding on to. I have forgiven myself and others. Forgiveness is an important part of accepting who I am, and coming to terms with the fact that I can't change my past, but I can determine my future. I am committed to loving me unconditionally! My past doesn't define my future.

I also realized that I have the power to find inner peace and control negative self-talk; doing so is a constant test. Sometimes I pass and other times I fail miserably. But, I am thankful to say, I am passing more often these days and continue to grow closer to being my best self. Changing my self-perception has been a key factor in my life changing process. "I am who I am and I be who I be. I LOVE ME!"

Fighting the negativity that had been poured into me over the years has not been easy. I discovered sources to pour different messages into myself, positive words, energy and thoughts. I began to listen to Les Brown cassette tapes, yes cassette tapes! Then I had the opportunity to serve as a publicity consultant for Iyanla Vanzant back in the 90's when she was producing motivational events in Harlem. Her message of empowerment was new to me, it was refreshing, perhaps even life changing, as it helped to chipped away at the negative inner voice.

During this time I spent 10 years as a consultant traveling across the United States and parts of the Caribbean as a part of African American Women On Tour (AAWOT) working for Maria Dowd. In this role I had the opportunity to meet many powerful women and hear their stories. I met Maya Angelou, Toni Morrison, Nikki Giovanni, Ruby Dee, Susan Taylor, Jewel Diamond Taylor, Queen Mutima Imani, Firayli Richmond and hundreds of women who were on their passion and purpose of empowerment.

Today I am sharing my truth, I am a work in progress! Shifting my energy continues to be an everyday part of my inner growth process. Each morning before I go out into the world I fill myself with a positive words, and affirmations. I start my day with prayer, then I listen to motivational videos on YouTube while I get ready for my day. Sometimes I meditate and exercise to get my positive energy flowing. I do my best to greet everyone with a smile and words of encouragement. I strive to pour love and positive energy into everyone I encounter, because this allows me to make a difference in my life and theirs.

I am creating a self-focused life shift which starts in my mind. By consciously and sub-consciously choosing to reinvent myself, I can automatically severe to empower family, friends and others through sharing my experiences, offering words of encouragement and coaching them to know their purpose and passion in life. This is my labor of love that I pray will have a ripple effect to empower positive change.

ABOUT

Portia Lockett

Everyone has a purpose, but not everyone knows their purpose early in life. At age seven, Portia Lockett was clear about her calling: teaching and encouraging others, which later evolved into her becoming a school teacher. After a lucrative career in media, she transitioned into speaking and training for major corporations including UAW GM, Chrysler, Women in Cable, the Detroit Area Agency on Aging, and The Detroit Medical Center.

Never afraid to make a change, Lockett became a licensed and ordained chaplain so she could support and encourage individuals from the cradle to the grave. She then embarked on international mission work that allowed her to travel and offer emotional and spiritual support in Japan, Barbados, Bahamas, and Jamaica.

Lockett's family became part of the *National Geographic* TV series *World Apart* where they lived an authentic lifestyle in the Andes with a Peruvian family.

She has been featured on CNN, in *The Michigan Chronicle*, *The Detroit News*, *Soul Source Magazine*, *Speakers Magazine*, on Radio One and in many online magazines and podcasts. Lockett also co-produced *Anointed Moments* a meditational CD and book.

Lockett is a living testimony to the survival and comeback spirit from the traumatic episodes in her life. From the loss of her father, surviving a divorce after almost twenty years of marriage, being diagnosed with several life-threatening diseases, foreclosure, bankruptcy, and unemployment. Overcoming these significant setbacks made Lockett the powerhouse speaker and sought after leader that she is today.

Website:	portialockett.com
Facebook:	Portia Lockett
Twitter:	@portialockett
LinkedIn:	portialockett
Email:	Portialockett2012@gmail.com
Phone:	313-307-9103

TOTAL PEACE!

By Portia Lockett

It was the summer of 1969 when someone took a Kodak picture of my elementary school sweetheart and me planting corn in the front of our Detroit school. Neither one of us could imagine at that moment that we would reconnect in high school, attend the prom together, and be partners on our senior trip. We didn't plan it but we both ended up attending Eastern Michigan University. It was during those college years that we became "serious' enough to break up and then make up and to explore all of the facets of "real" love. After graduation we settled into our careers. We traveled on a regular basis, viewing the world and its varying cultures together. Fast forward to the year 1988; a year full of brand new beginnings. My childhood sweetheart and I entered into holy matrimony and gave birth to our firstborn son. Later on after deep conversation we were led to become foster parents to an amazing thirteen year old. And as the years passed, we gave birth to two more sons, culminating in our beautiful household of six.

We were for sure a very happy couple, stable in our careers, spiritually sound, financially secure, and well connected with community. Our home was always the gathering place for family and friends. They were present for our jamming in July parties, Kwanzaa celebrations, birthday festivities, sister circle prayer sessions, basketball competitions, and late nights of chilling in the Jacuzzi under the stars.

During all those amazing years, Luther was always singing in my ear, *"Still in love, still in love with you!"*

Then, exactly ten calendar days following America's 9/11 tragedy, I experienced my very own life changing episode! The perfectly sculpted mosaic of my life changed drastically.

I was conducting a corporate training session when I got a call from my husband. He was inquiring about our weekend plans because my cousins from Chicago were coming to town. In a rush to return to my session, I abruptly ended the call and promised to call him later during a short break.

When I called back he didn't answer. I was a little anxious because I knew that I had only a few moments to talk. That's when it happened. I heard in my head, a voice say, *"Your family was in an accident."* I dismissed it not only because I had just spoken to him, but because this was not how I normally heard the *Holy Spirit* speak to me. But I put it out of my mind and finished my session.

Later I discovered several messages from the Detroit Police Department stating that I needed to get to the hospital immediately because there had been a serious accident involving my family and a drunk driver. *My stomach dropped.*

Driving with my heart in my throat, I arrived at the hospital to find my husband, sons, and godson, in the emergency room. Although the boys were stable my *"Still in love. Still in love with,"* husband had suffered a broken pelvis, a damaged heart, collapsed lungs, and broken ribs. During the weeks that he was in the hospital I posted healing scriptures and the cards he'd received on the walls of his hospital room. I didn't want to leave his side so this meant the working and the traveling that provided much of our income came to a screeching halt and eventually our savings were depleted.

One day, I was sitting in the lobby returning phones calls and I noticed a mother leaving with a newborn. God spoke to me and told me to bless her with what I had in my pocket. I had $20.00, literally, the last of our savings. I was obedient and I offered it to the young mother. She looked at me in surprise then shared that she didn't know how she was going to buy diapers and had prayed asking God to help her. By the time I got home, one of my best friends, who had just started her own company, gave me a check from her first client and said, you're going to need this. By blessing others I had been blessed. This was the beginning of living in the overflow. Every day for several months, people offered financial blessings. I went home to envelopes in my mailbox with checks. The benefits and promises of tithing kicked in with full force.

Weeks later after awakening from a medically induced coma, doctors discovered that my husband had sustained a closed head injury. This was the beginning of the end of our BLISS! The man I loved and married no longer existed. His head injury changed him in ways I could never have imagined. I wanted to find the drunk driver who caused this trauma, the one I thought responsible for the complete and total disruption of our beautiful family. *I was furious!*

The man I'd known for over thirty years was **GONE**... My husband had changed. Depression set in, and he was always angry and in constant pain. There were many seemingly uncontrollable outbursts where he would yell at me and our boys. He no longer allowed me to support him during his medical visits with physicians, psychiatrists, and psychologists. At this point I felt completely useless and detached. There were nights when he didn't even come home. That's when the affairs and emotional abuse started. It was all beyond stressful. The last straw was when I saw his fist come within centimeters of my face to leave a hole in the hallway wall. I was being chased around our bedroom in the middle of the night! The place that had once been our sacred space was now a den of unrest. I got tired of sleeping with a hammer for protection from my own husband. I told him if he didn't get additional help he had to leave. When he responded that *I WAS THE ONE* who needed help. I realized that he was right. *I DID NEED HELP* and started seeing a therapist. Fortunately my therapist was able to help me understand the impact of the trauma to his brain. She shared that the damage had caused major changes, leaving no filter in his thought process. The only thing that seemed to help was the prescribed medication that he hated taking because of how it made him feel.

I had a choice to make: either allow my sons to continue to witness the abuse and unacceptable behavior and think it was normal, or separate from my husband and try to guide three young sons into manhood by myself. I made the wisest choice, I chose to declare my own sanity and peace of mind. At night when my sons went to sleep, I would often remind God of His word, I would say with boldness: "God you said," and follow it up with scriptures. I would pull out my bible and recite scriptures that gave me strength. There were a few that really kept me sustained. Philippians 4:13 *I can do all things through Christ that strengthens me. Isaiah 54:17 No weapons that have been formed against me shall prosper* and the entire Psalms 91. I committed to daily affirmations: *No matter what it looks like, feels like, or sounds like, all is in divine order!* I would play Yolanda Adams' *"The Battle is Not Yours!"* And lots of other uplifting music. I also started working out and this helped me to stay focused and gave me back my appetite, which had diminished.

At church, I placed myself on the altar for prayer. I cried and prayed my way through this horrific experience. There was no way out, I had to keep walking until I could see the light of day again. Our country was broken and so was I. Our country had suffered a great loss and I had lost my husband. Several times I cried out asking God, "why me?" What had I done to deserve this? I was the person always advising others on how to handle life issues, interceding for them in prayer and telling them to **WATCH GOD!** And I was lost.

The only thing I knew to do was to pray. I was led to reach out to my extended family and individuals who asked what they could do to help me on this journey. I decided to be transparent. It felt so much better to release all that I had contained for so long. My sister circle, their godparents, my biological family, my church family, and my closest friends all stepped up to the plate. I also met with my sons' teachers, principals and sports coaches for their support for the boys, because of the affect the situation was having on their education. I eventually scheduled family counseling as well as individual sessions so my sons could voice their feelings. I did everything I knew to do in order to get us through what appeared to be a never-ending nightmare.

I prayed for peace.

My husband and I had been separated now for approximately six months and I just knew he would get the help he desperately needed and we would eventually get back to some normalcy. But that didn't happen…. He was no longer the man I had married. The closed head injury had made him a different person.

When I was served divorce papers on October 31, 2006 I thought, *Is this a trick or a treat?* It was neither. It was a reality that had to be faced so I could move forward. I was so embarrassed, and just like many other women, I didn't share this with a lot of people because I didn't want to be judged. Here I was a spiritual advisor, a chaplain, and partner in a flourishing business, but my life had shattered into pieces.

Regardless of my circumstance, I kept my faith and I gained an unshakable trust in God! I knew everything was going to be all right!

It's been ten years, and after much soul searching, support from my family, extended family, and deep prayer, I forgave my former husband for the decisions that he made. I've also forgiven the drunk driver who caused the permanent disruption in our lives. Even though I never even knew his name.

I realized I had to let go of something from the past to gain something greater for my future. I can now move forward and share my story with others. I was tried, now I'm able to testify. I can tell the whole truth because I feel at TOTAL PEACE! It was delayed but not denied!

Now that I am healed and delivered from the spiritual, mental, and emotional rollercoaster. I am waiting patiently for God to allow me to be found as a Proverbs 31 woman in waiting for her Boaz.

ABOUT

Yolanda M. Billings

With more than thirty years working in the financial services industry, Yolanda M. Billings, has provided tax, accounting, and investment services to many individuals and small businesses through her company Y.M.B. and Associates LLC.

In 2009 she formed, One Common Goal, a nonprofit organization—dedicated to financial literacy and entrepreneurism—to encourage people to look at entrepreneurism as a way of life and a means to financial security and independence.

With a mission of providing financial literacy, the organization attempts to address the needs of the community by providing education through seminars, workshops, and networking.

Over the past seven years Yolanda has partnered with the Benevolent Tax Professional Services Inc. as a V.I.T.A. participant, to help train volunteers and provide free tax preparation services for low income individuals and seniors within the Queens area.

Address:	Y.M.B. and Associates 224-02 Linden Blvd Cambria Heights, NY 11411
Website:	ymbassociates.com
Phone:	718-527-0206
Fax:	718-527-3102

DON'T LOOK BACK BECAUSE THE FUTURE IS MUCH BRIGHTER

By Yolanda Billings

We were born into a world whose message was that life and all of its successes were ours "for the taking." We were told that if we had a happy childhood, did well in school, and graduated from college, we would find a "good" job, an understanding and supporting mate, and have 2.5 children, live in a house with a white picket fence, *and* a dog!

In our parents' day, life was more predictable. People lived by the concept of putting God first, family second, and job third. They hoped to enjoy— or at least tolerate—their job, and then retire, and after having earned the right, they'd enjoy the fruits of their labor. And, because of the love and support given to their children and other family members, they were assured to always be cared for… to the very end.

Unfortunately, life and the world we now live in, are not cooperating with this vision of our future. Education has become extremely expensive, and graduating from a good college with even a 4.0 average, no longer guarantees the job you may want or need. Relationships are no longer expected to last "'til death do us part," and many family gatherings are limited to funerals and weddings.

Rather than believing we can take hold of our lives, many of us allow others to dictate their ideas about *our* abilities, values and successes. Life is a game, and many of us have lost the will to win.

In order to survive in this economy you must take control of your life. It is crucial to make use of support groups to gather the skills, information, and contacts you need. Never be too proud to ask for help, or work with people who genuinely want to work with you.

And remember... always take time out for yourself and those close to you... never let anyone rob you of your "faith" or take away your focus.

When I wrote the passage above "not so long ago," I was discouraged, angry, and desperately in search of self. I was working for a company under a manager who made it clear that his goal was to "get rid of" all female managers in his downline, and retire all seasoned personnel to create a newer version of his kingdom.

For many years I truly enjoyed my job, my staff and my industry. But, after the events of 9/11, life changed for all of us. In addition to the loss of family and friends, those fruitful years of the late 90's were gone. Companies lost money, had to reorganize and eliminate anything and anyone that was considered dead weight. As companies downsized, many of those who remained, found themselves performing the job of two or three people. They dared not complain realizing that there were others who needed a job. Life was changing fast, and if you were unwilling to change with it, you were going to be left behind.

In the 1990's we laughed at the need for Google and were upset that Apple's price wasn't moving. But embracing the need and opportunity for change, these two companies have not only survived, but thrived. Today, many of us have come to not only enjoy, but depend on their services. And yes, this change has helped many to become successful and wealthy.

After sixteen years of loyal productive service I found that the upper management I was accustomed to, had either retired or had passed away. I could no longer pick up the phone and directly call a portfolio manager, a vice president, or even the president. The company I had grown to love no longer felt like a family it now felt like a "job."

This was a time for reflection. I needed to take control of my life and make use of support groups to gather the skills, information, and the contacts I needed. And I had to stop being too proud to ask for help, or work with people who genuinely wanted to work with me...to be honest, I'm still working on that last part.

After being comfortable with my position, my income, my office (with a window), I decided to leave corporate and step out completely on my own. This however, was not easy to do. I had to expand my tax office to accommodate my other businesses; which meant a larger space, more rent, more utilities, more furniture, more supplies and more money to accomplish it. I also had to get used to not having regular checks deposited into my account on payday, because I no longer had a regular payday. But I survived!

As scary as this change was I had to adapt. I had to learn and embrace new technology. I had to be willing to learn new ideas, and concepts along with the ever changing laws and rules within my craft. And I had to accept these changes... even though I may not have seen the need for them.

Being an entrepreneur lets you work on your own terms; you keep your own money and pick and choose who you want to work with. You set the goals, the vision, and the pace. But you also have to do the work. You can *easily* spend many more hours working on your own than you ever did as an employee. But it makes you a more confident person, and it's worth all the work!

We spend so much time and effort refusing to change. We talk about the good old days... how simple they were, how easy they were, and how happy we were. I don't know about you, but I don't want to go back to black and white television, or the $169.75 per week I made on my first job. And as much as I fought against getting a cell phone in the 90's... I am not willing to give it up now.

If we want to make more money, or accomplish our idea of success, we must be willing to place ourselves in a position to do so. The most powerful way to do this it to network.

Networking, as defined by the Merriam Webster Dictionary is: "The exchange of information or services among individuals, groups, or institutions; specifically: the cultivation of productive relationships for employment or business."

Networking with people who have to rely on their own resources to survive can be encouraging and motivating. Every business is different and everyone has their own ideas. Meeting with these individuals can help you learn new ways of doing business or of handling ourselves in business situations. You might even be able to help someone else increase to improve their business activities. Networking is a two-way street. You must be willing to *give*, in order to *get*. It may seem uncomfortable in the beginning, but in time it becomes second nature.

Setting up a support network when you are unemployed is also important. You'll benefit from the encouragement, and new viewpoints others may be able to provide. They may also continue to mentor you during your new employment to provide emotional support and continued peace of mind.

Despite the challenges you may face, you will never be in a better position to achieve financial security for yourself and your family. The future is unchartered and waiting to be explored. And... although you should never forget your past... you don't have to drag it with you!

ABOUT

Natalie Bennett

Natalie has spent the majority of her life as an accomplished licensed esthetician for a major cosmetic company. She is also a world-renowned visual stylist and makeup artist. Her specialty has been to determine and create the perfect look for clients to enhance their ultimate individual beauty. Various events and circumstances in Natalie's life lead her to focus less on the physical aspects and ramifications of beauty and more on the spiritual/soul aspects of beauty.

Currently Natalie is a Wellness Motivation Strategist who believes that true beauty starts on the inside with a balance of healthy mind, body, and spirit. Natalie believes that by taking full accountability for your life, practicing forgiveness, and remaining consciously diligent of what you allow inside your body as well as your mind, you're destined to become your most beautiful self. Natalie teaches women to redefine the essence of beauty from the inside to out and believes that when you truly feel beautiful at the core of your spirit/soul, the outside persona is sure to follow.

Emails:	Natalieb3chi@gmail.com
	4thenatureofwellness@gmail.com
Facebook:	natalie.brown.56863
Instagram:	grateful4chi

A JOURNEY TO HEALING, SELF-DISCOVERY AND REINVENTION

By Natalie Bennett

It's December 2006, I had just turned thirty-nine and was a newlywed going into my third marriage. Life was seemingly flowing smoothly with family and a career as a lead esthetician and makeup artist for a well-known cosmetic company. The Friday before Christmas, my husband and I were off work spending time at home with our daughter. I was due any day with my second child, while my first child was almost a year-and-a-half old. He decided to go to the grocery store to pick up a few things to make for breakfast. I stayed home with our daughter. Twenty minutes later the doorbell rang, and to my surprise it was a police officer handing me my husband's car keys and informing me that he was under arrest. The officer stated some immigration code violations to me then handed me a business card with a number on it to call for information. I was in complete shock but was absolutely sure that it had to be a mistake.

Back then, under the Bush Administration there was a law, soon to be passed, that if any immigrant had been in the United States five years or more but had not established legal citizenship they could *not* be legally deported. There were protests around the country as thousands of immigrants were taken from families, arrested, rounded up, and deported before the law could be passed. My husband who is originally from Nigeria, had been in the U.S. for many years but unbeknown to me, he was still considered an illegal alien because of incomplete paperwork. The stress from my husband's arrest sent me into early labor. I gave birth to our second daughter two days before Christmas. Three months later after consulting with lawyer after lawyer trying to have my husband released, he was still deported back to Nigeria. Each immigration lawyer that I spoke with advised me that the quickest way to legally get my husband back into the country was to go to Nigeria and file for an appeal with the American Embassy there. Now, I'd never dated a Black American. My first husband was Caucasian and my second husband was a West African Senegalese Prince. Although the Senegalese swore to never practiced polygamy like his Muslim leader father that had seven wives, he certainly made his way around. My grandmother would often joke and say that when I was ready for a Brotha I went straight to the motherland.

Terrified and excited I packed up and moved to the Motherland, Lagos, Nigeria, to be exact. My two daughters were at the time six months and two years old. When I got there, Lagos seemed like an African version of New York; running on pure adrenaline from chaos and confusion. About a month after moving my family into my eldest sister-in-law's home, an advertisement on television caught my attention for an upcoming Lagos Fashion Week. I noticed that Nigerians were very fashionable and into makeup so I decided to take my chances and call the number advertised. As a result of making that phone call one thing led to another and before I knew it I was launching and orchestrating a cosmetic line for two wealthy Nigerian sisters. I became their general manager and structured and implemented everything for our new company based on my fifteen years of experiences with cosmetic companies in the United States. In a very short time the business skyrocketed to success with distributors and stores all over Africa.

Within that year I started a modeling agency under the same umbrella, which allowed us to participate in major fashion and entertainment events featuring many American celebrities. During this time the company was thriving, but my life at home was a different story. My husband struggled to find work to help support our growing family; by this time I was expecting our third daughter. During my pregnancy he became increasingly more physically, psychologically, and emotionally abusive. After giving birth to my daughter in the back seat of our SUV, I was surprised that I was not asked by the paramedics why I was covered in belt marks except on my stomach where I was able to shield him from hitting me.

As the representative for the cosmetic line my presence became more in demand, which fueled his abusive fire even more. During the third year of living in Nigeria my husband tried his best to sabotage any and everything that made me successful. None of his actions made sense to me, especially since I was the sole reason we were surviving. I felt completely broken down to nothing, so I started drinking alcohol to numb myself. Unfortunately my girls were witnesses to most of the physical abuse and I was hospitalized a few times as a result. Coming up on the fourth year I was employed, but barely. We lived below poverty and were struggling to make ends meet. To save my children as well as myself, I knew I needed to plan our escape back to America.

During my four years in Africa I was told by numerous Nigerian women that they would never have left their own country, family, friends, or culture to follow a man! That said, I am a true believer that everything happens for a reason. The good experiences as well as the bad are essential for us to learn and grow as individuals. What doesn't kill you for DAMN sure makes you stronger. I now know my strengths and power as a woman and a mother. By the grace of God I was able to return home to the United States in August 2011 without my husband. Upon my arrival, I began an amazing spiritual journey of healing, forgiveness, discovery, and reinvention.

Now that I am spiritually in tune to self, I can live my life and see the world through eyes of gratitude. I may have been spiritually delayed but never spiritually denied.

FINAL WORDS

We hope that you were empowered by the stories we have shared with you. We believe that they have the ability to change your life. We are sure that while reading some of them you probably thought about your own story. Let's face it, we've all experienced a setback that positioned us for a comeback. We would like to invite you to participate in our third anthology, *Delayed But Not Denied: Book 3*. If you're interested in becoming a part of our next bestselling book project, please contact us at **www.delayedbutnotdenied.info**

Additionally, you may be interested in your own book anthology project for you and your tribe. If you would like us to assist you with creating a book compilation for you and your network contact us. If you are also interested in writing and publishing your own book, we can help there as well. Either way, you should contact us so we can discuss how we can assist you in making your author dreams come true. You can reach either Toni or Julia by emailing **admin@delayedbutnotdenied.info** or calling us at **646-421-0830** or **917-501-6780**.

NOTES